A Philosophy
of Literature

Raymond Tschumi

DUFOUR EDITIONS
Philadelphia
1968

LIBRARY OF CONGRESS CATALOG CARD No. 62: 12798

Second Printing 1968

PRINTED IN GREAT BRITAIN FOR DUFOUR EDITIONS

CONTENTS

PART I

THE LITERARY REALITY

CONTENTS

PART II

THE MAKING OF LITERATURE

CONTENTS

PART III

IN THE OPEN HEART

THE subject-matter of this book is of less importance than the method and the approach to the subject-matter. This book is neither an introduction to literature nor a theory of literature; it is a study of the relations between mind and facts, of the literary reality (Part One), of the creative way of looking at things (Part Two), and of the continuity and wholeness of meaning (Part Three).

My main philosophical postulate is that facts or feelings are real only when they correspond to each other. It follows that literature, which serves as a link between facts and feelings, may be chosen as the starting point of a theory of reality (as in Part One), creates its own reality (as I try to show in Part Two) and implies the continuity of time as well as the plenitude of life (to which I point in Part Three).

We are here not to discover worlds, but to make them, and whatever we may do depends on our hands, our machines, our mind and our heart. In the deep freedom of our spirit lies the perpetual possibility, the fire that burns our mortal lives, that makes and destroys whatever is allowed to exist for a while. My inquiry stops where the mystery begins. But the mystery is ours and dwells in us. *I* can do no more. Whatever may happen to us will spring from us, and whatever will be, will be made and unmade by the spirit. Nothing is strong, nothing lasts, except time itself, and time is a coincidence of patience and events, of faith and realities, of hope and miseries, of truth and disillusions. Truth will never be found here, caught and solidified. Truth is time, and lasts, even now. There is no end, no ultimate interpretation.

Everyone knows in his heart that, because time is continuous, it is vain to imagine a transcendental eternity outside time. What passes may be despised, but not the passing. Duration is brotherhood and reality is meaning; these two statements sum up the positive side of my philosophy of literature : it is very little. Philosophers have little to contribute to human welfare; always searching for and testing their truth, they are supposed to lose touch with realities. And yet they are more influential, more in touch with realities and—as the case may be—more dangerous than business men, statesmen or scientists, for they look behind what passes, into duration. They rarely hit the mark, often build wooden systems, and always play with fire. They cannot say what truth is; they make it as writers of fiction do, and they often make it in the wrong way. The less they affirm, the better. Perhaps the only truth is that there is a truth, and the philosopher's task is to look for it, not to discover it once for all, for truth changes with men and techniques. The truth of our industrial society is not the truth of the Church in the Middle Ages, and the truth of all books fades away, except for what is always present and living.

It is as important to criticize one's statements as it is to state anything. It is more difficult to criticize philosophy than literature, and therefore criticism is less developed in philosophy. It should be the other way round, for the critical mind tests the products of thought, their relations to facts and to the soul, their adherence to truth, in one word their life. Criticism expels dead words and restores meaning, but then no thought is left; life prevails and life is meaning.

There remains for me the pleasant task of acknowledging my debt of gratitude towards those who helped me in my work. Miss Helen Bächtiger typed the whole manuscript with an astonishing accuracy; Dr. Siegfried Wyler read a first draft and made valuable suggestions; Mr. Thomas Lindsay carefully and competently corrected errors in phrases and vocabulary; finally Mr. Douglas Gillam made additional suggestions. To all of them I express my sincere thanks.

St. Gallen, 1960.

PART ONE

The Literary Reality

1. PHILOSOPHY OF LITERATURE VERSUS
HISTORICAL CRITICISM

WE assume the possibility and admit the existence of a philosophy of history, but we never speak of a philosophy of literature, although literature, like history, is an interpretation of life, and has a history. Even such a relatively young literature as the American literature has its histories, not to speak of individual authors, who have their manners and periods. Those who die young are dismissed as unaccountable geniuses, until they belong to a posthumous school.

Originating in oral tradition, literature has served in turn as an entertainment for princes, as a national glory or as a pastime for leisured ladies, as a red flag for angry citizens and as a solace for pious souls. Literary history has become a complement to social history, a kind of history of taste, influenced by changes in religion, science and politics.

Literary history is certainly a justified and well-established science, but its very 'taken-for-grantedness', if the word may be permitted, has prevented us from venturing to explore in another direction. Is not the written word, of all human aspirations, the one which has most claims to eternity? Does it not defy time? Is it not strange that, though ideas change, they should leave monuments, some of which are still unforgotten, ready to receive a fresh interpretation? Does it not strike the reader of literary histories that there is something in really great works that escapes the historical approach, whereas less valuable writings are easily dealt with?

All those I have met who have seen either Lascaux or Altamira have been deeply impressed by the permanent language of their cave paintings; this also is a written work, the earliest that we know.

Permanence, and not change, is the essential character of literature, and should be the focus and the aim of our efforts. Why do we prefer to study what passes away, that is, the mortal element? What pleasure that is obscure, sad and sadistic do we find in such obstinate grave-digging?

La Chanson de Roland is perhaps not the greatest of poems. If critics compare it with Homer, it is mainly because both authors are conjectural or because it may have originated in an oral tradition, and then been transcribed by one or several scribes for the pilgrims. Its ideal is the ideal of chivalry, which is buried. The problem has been : when and how and for whom it was composed.

Beowulf is a much better target for historians because its ideals are as dark as the Saxon woods, whereas the historical and philological materials are a rich vein.

A last instance : the proportion in the Chaucer bibliography between what has been written on Chaucer, the man, his times and his language, on the one hand, and the meaning of his work for the twentieth-century reader on the other hand, is as 91 to 9 (I hope I exaggerate).

After all this, who will venture to look for anything permanent? We are so much obsessed with time that, out of jealousy and meanness, we want to destroy the few monuments of that most unknown and unreal nonentity : thought. Our way to the permanent past is encumbered with the litter of time, and we are constantly looking for more litter in order to hide the monument.

Fortunately, on this side of the iron curtain, we have not

gone so far as voluntarily to believe, under penalty of unrecorded deportation, that the spirit is a reflection from matter. That old god, matter, is able to emit very harmful rays, but has never produced a single breath of spirit.

Who (again) will venture? Unless the first one be great, he will have to rely upon mighty precedents. The century of Theophile Gautier and Oscar Wilde is the first that comes to my mind. Examples are to be found in almost every century, especially in the reflections of poets upon their art. The present century, perhaps because we live and fear in it, seems to provide little to strengthen our belief in permanence. It is a century of little confidence and of hasty writing, while Homer is stored, I suppose, by the Americans, in the form of microphotographic copies, well under the roots of life.

Gautier's permanence, however, has nothing soft or thrilling about it:

> *"Tout passe. L'art robuste*
> *Seul a l'éternité;*
> *Le buste*
> *Survit à la cité."*

It should not be inferred that a philosophy of literature presupposes an essentially permanent literature. I only want to define the limits of the historical approach.

To change our attitude to literature, I propose that what is essential in literature, the spirit (and not the word) should be regarded as a nonentity, as unreal. Realities pass away. Let us leave things and objects for the scientist: we are dealing with the ideal non-existent spirit, absent from the world but present in man, in the subject.

The first question I am always asked about my poetry is: "What is it about?" I am unable to answer because it is precisely about nothing (here the reader should not mistake " nothing" for Mallarméan nothingness), so that those who are looking for stars, mud and roses, or the locomotive engine forced into poetry by Stephen Spender, will find joy and re-nunciation, plenitude and loneliness; the stars and engines are dissolved in the acids of the mind.

The study of 'background' and the minute classification of words and works is useful, but their opacity has hidden more vital issues. We usually shun the spirit because it is fire, and it cannot be touched. We know it would burn our dry and cold, objective and prudent, sluggish intellects. So we sleep, dream-ing of the haunting images, and when we wake in the morning we announce that Shakespeare is great; because this is a safe statement.

Fire cannot be touched; it throws a light on things around it, but what is important is neither the wood nor the glowing object with its shadows, but the warmth.

Am I then excluding reality from my projected philosophy of literature? To use once more the image of the fire, it is no more to be excluded than the wood from the fire. I emphasize only that the problem lies in the *relation* between reality and the spirit.

Any philosophy of literature that deals with its proper 'object', the spirit, will have to acknowledge features which have no affinity with external facts. To permanence we some-times add universality. Yeats writes of tragedy: "The persons upon the stage, let us say, greaten till they are humanity it-self".[1] Montaigne's *Essays* inform us about one particular man, but *"Tout homme porte en soi la forme entière de l'humaine condition"*.

At this point, we can see clearly that a philosophy of litera-ture would be quite opposite to the philosophy of nature, not in its methods and results perhaps, but in its object, because literature is a relation between the spirit and the world, whereas nature is matter, and yet matter seems now to be such a wonderfully subtle thing as to become almost spiritual. Never-theless, common sense teaches us that *'fugit irreparabile tempus'*, that things—and the body—appear, grow, decay

[1] *Essays*, p. 303 ; The Tragic Theatre, London, 1934.

and disappear. Change is the law of limited things. They wait only for a definition. The spirit, on the contrary, cannot be defined, because it has no limits. Ideas and emotions may change the form into which they are cast, but they can use many moulds, some of which are invested with a perdurable and universal meaning.

If a philosophy of literature wishes to deal with the undefinable, the immeasurable, the ungraspable, the unreal, is its task possible? Before we answer this question, it will be useful to examine some of the philosophies of art.

In the century of Auguste Comte and Ernest Renan it was possible for Hippolyte Taine to announce that *"les vertus et les vices sont des produits comme le vitriol et le sucre"*, to deduce La Fontaine from his background, to write *De l'Intelligence,* a book showing that, from the reflexes to the most abstract ideas, all our activities depend on the material environment, and to write a *Philosophy of Art* in which art (the same applies to literature, as in Taine's *History of English Literature*) is shown to be a mere product of time.

The value of Taine's works is undeniable, and the champions of historical criticism or dialectic materialism would do well not to forget him altogether. I am not concerned, however, with the genial application of his doctrine, but with the ultimates of his conception of art, literature, and the mind.

If art is a distorted imitation of nature (I am aware that this tradition originates with Aristotle, that formidable cataloguer) and a product of circumstances, then art is no more than an imperfect document. Perfection, supreme values and reality are to be found in nature or in society: " Art is the product of society, as the pearl is the product of the oyster, and to stand outside art is to stand inside society." This statement by Christopher Caudwell (*Illusion and Reality,* Macmillan, 1937, XIV), a champion of dialectic materialism, reminds us of Taine's *"le vice et la vertu sont des produits comme le vitriol et le sucre."* Here is Caudwell's conclusion :

"Communist poetry will be complete, because it will be man conscious of his own necessity as well as that of outer reality." Indeed! It is not surprising that Taine should have secretly elaborated a theory of atoms, for the key to mystery (or absence of knowledge) must in his eyes have dwelt there (he was also the author of thirteen sonnets on his cats, in the manner of Lecomte de Lisle).

It follows from all this that, from the *mantis religiosa* (praying mantis) to God through the spirit, everything is a product of matter, which is given the more noble name of substance: *"La cause des actes finis du monde est la substance en tant qu'on la considère comme ayant déjà produit Dieu."*[2] Curiously enough, but this is a logical consequence of the system, the law of causation stops there: *"Tout a une cause, hormis la substance et ses attributs."*[3] Such is the metaphysics of materialism. It leads to an utterly inhuman, tyrannical and mysterious absolute in face of which we become hysterical, knowing that Her Majesty the Substance will not care about our nervous or, to go down to a still lower level, spiritual agitations and titillations. Compared to Substance, the fierce gods of the tribes, the jungle and the bloody temples are but a masquerade of amateurs. Here we have that totalitarian absolute, too well known in the twentieth century, from whom even God has to ask for bread.

At least the gods leave the tribes in peace when the victims have been sacrificed, but from the causing cause there is no escape, no freedom, no peace, only the security of being caused and destroyed. That absolute, taught to millions of poor workers, will immolate all men who have been foolish and logical enough to have an idea of it, because there is no escape . . .

The whole system also, conceived by thinkers impatiently looking, in patient works, for objective truth, relies on a wrong notion of objectivity. The whole system is a creation of the

[2] *H. Taine, sa Vie et sa Correspondance,* Paris, Hachette, 1902, p. 351.
[3] Ibidem p. 300.

mind although it originates in the observation of the *mantis religiosa,* and as such is subjective, in spite of its scientific basis. Contemporary scientists understand causation better. In any event, whatever the scientists and philosophers may believe the world to be, it is their mind that provides the fiction as to the system.

In literature, philosophy has its place, but it is the content and the form of ideas that matter, rather than the world they represent. The creative power of the spirit and neither the cause nor the object, is the leading force at work, and it happens that the more freely the spirit acts, the truer the work is. What and where substance is, matters very little. We shall probably never know, but I am convinced that there is something substantial in the spirit, whether human or divine, real or unreal. The only thing I want to suggest is that substance, or matter, or nature, or God is an objective entity only insofar as it is conceived by us, the subject. Objectivity is a relative notion. There is a support for our conclusion in Taine's contradictory metaphysics : *"La Pensée est conçue par soi."*[4] The supreme, the ultimate object is an attribute of that which conceives, of the spirit, and so the circle goes round, leading nowhere else than to itself, whenever we follow the line.

One consequence of absolute objectivism is that literature has been viewed from the point of view of the scientist and dealt with as if it were a *mantis religiosa* : when the head is cut off, the tail keeps moving.[5]

[4] Ibidem, p. 300.
Taine, *De l'Intelligence,* Tome Premier, Paris, Hachette (no date) P. 353 "Qu'on en détache encore la tête, et le segment isolé vivra . . ."

2. FACTS AND FICTION

THE title *Reality in Literature,* which I had first applied to Part One, may mislead readers into believing that works of fiction, or imaginative literature, should be excluded from this survey. Not so. On the contrary, fiction represents an inner reality, which is at least as significant as the outer world. The essence of fiction, indeed, is the meaning, for the fictitious characters, plot and scenery, however true or likely they may seem, exist only in relation to the meaning. Each poet, novelist and dramatist also aims more or less expressly at representing things which his readers can recognize, but his chief purpose is to move, to provoke a reaction to the fictitious data, and this reaction *is* the meaning of the work, it is a reaction to a supposed, artificially created reality, which is none the less a true substitute for reality. The study of this reaction, of the meaning of the work, belongs to the philosophy of literature, it is a study of awareness, a discernment of consciousness.

For what is reality in itself? No reality exists by itself and for itself, and those realities of which we are aware exist only as a product of our awareness. At least for any work of literature, reality (the external or psychological reality) exists only as a support for the meaning. To give a concrete example, there are many unrecorded storms, but a given storm becomes worth recording when it is conceived as a symbol, or when it provokes fear, or when it is related to a meaningful plot (as in so many poems, plays, novels, musical compositions and paintings, which it would take too long to enumerate). Rossini's Overture to *William Tell,* or the storm in Beethoven's *Sixth Symphony* are good examples of nature transformed into art. We do not care about the reality of those storms : the reality lies within the listeners; even the sounds, the drums and the rhythm are music, and not a 'real' or physical storm. And indeed, only a small part of music is imitative. As for literature, although it has at its disposal more accurate means of describing nature, it rarely and exceptionally reaches the closeness of the scientific approach, which, whatever its discoveries may be, will only grasp what can be grasped : the fact eludes the mind, and the mind takes from nature what can be given back to the mind. Mere reality and mere facts are irreducible and meaningless; this explains our anguish and fear before the forever unexplained objective world and its unaccountable passing and growing. And yet consciousness is there, whether we like it or not, and the least gifted of us attributes a meaning to that world, so that the meaninglessness and the mere facts shrink away; everything lives dimly within ourselves, and something is centred upon ourselves, until it finds its expression in the work of art.

3. OBJECTIVITY

THESE are subjective views which will be attributed—quite erroneously—to a partial philosophy. Few words are more misleading than 'subjective' and 'objective', with their corelatives of 'realism', 'positivism', 'idealism' and 'naturalism'. Neither the subject nor the object can destroy its opposite, and sometimes what, from one point of view, is the subject becomes, from another point of view, the object, so that these words have little philosophical relevance. For practical purposes, the psychologists have to make an object out of the psyche, which is essentially subjective; that this can be done is a proof of the relativity of these concepts.

When I emphasize that science, our most objective activity, is a progressive assimilation of objective facts, I mean that this objectivity is a practical device, the essential method. This does not imply that the remotest stars or the smallest phenomena of the atom have no relation to us or stand apart as, essentially, objects. The distinction belongs to the mind, not to nature. Distinction, separation, and limitation, whether social, scientific or psychological, originate in the mind. This book is made of sentences, but the world, if the world exists, is made of one sentence. This is why the best works of art obey the supreme law of art, the law of unity. Because science is objective, it need not give a sense of plenitude, but that is the duty of art and of literature, which have to assimilate reality, to transform it into human experience.

Here we might pause a while in order to show the pointlessness—except for a practical purpose—of the quarrel between objectivism and subjectivism. We quote a passage from Whitehead's *Science and the Modern World*.[1]

"My second reason for distrusting subjectivism is based on the particular content of experience. Our historical knowledge tells us of ages in the past when, so far as we can see, no living being existed on earth. Again it also tells us of countless star-systems, whose detached history remains beyond our ken". We may argue: what is that objective world which lies outside our grasp? Where is the proof that it is not reflected in some subconscious way? Is it not objective merely because it is unknown? But the most serious objection is that the possibilities of the subject are also infinite, unknown and unrecorded. We agree with Whitehead that objectivity is necessary to the scientist, but it is obvious that subjectivity, though with an inevitable proportion of objectivity, is necessary to the creator of a work of art, because the latter does not, as the scientist does, leave reality outside, but has to assume it and to work it out with the real tools of his mind.

The trouble with Whitehead, and with all those who take the scientist's point of view, is that they invariably suppose, without questioning the validity of their hypothesis, that reality *is* outside, and that truth is simply a more or less faithful account of that external world.

I have sufficiently demonstrated that the external character of reality is relative. Bergson was better able to grasp the essence of art, as he was aware that the intellect, whose function is to analyse, is unable to comprehend the wholeness of duration, a reality that is to be found in art. With intuition, or the perception of things in duration, reality is inside, and in art reality is life, neither outside nor inside, but both. The complex, harmonious sentence, as opposed to the mere juxtaposition or superposition of abstract, separated concepts, is that which 'catches' reality: the character of wholeness and unity is stressed, together with the importance of style (for style is the ordering of intuitions).

[1] Cambridge University Press, 1953, p. 111.

This discussion leads to an examination of the origins of abstraction and language. Here also it is generally supposed that they are to be found outside, and I have shown that the hypothesis may be practical and useful, but does not hold true after a closer scrutiny. The word 'tree' does not originate in the tree, but in the mind. Language is expression as well as impression. An abstraction such as the word 'reality' (from the Latin *res*—thing) represents the choice of a general element, and it is true to say both that it is a choice, that is, an act of the mind, and that it is an abstract word, that is, a word applying to many concrete words and things.

When we come to the study of atomic motions, we are forced to express them in mathematical symbols and relations which are abstraction at a high level. But again these symbols are neither subjective nor objective : they are both. In spite of all the instruments of research, our observations will not go deeper if the mind does not provide the necessary means of understanding the facts. There must be a certain relation between the strangest phenomena and the human mind. The very words 'phenomena', 'object', 'facts', 'processes' suggest an attitude of objectivity, passivity, indifference, impartiality which is that of the scientist. They are dry words, without any human warmth (except 'phenomenon', which may at times imply a sense of mystery).

The attitude of the scientist towards what he observes is the right one, but it is a singularly limited attitude to life. It is not surprising that many physicists should have given proof of complete insensitivity, human irresponsibility and moral indifference in regard to atomic fission and fusion.

This attitude has degenerated into materialism, and has built a society based upon a material scale of values, in which the dry calculators are the successful men, and material prosperity is the aim. It is a society for facts and abstractions, not for men.

The same attitude has been dignified, sublimated and generalized into a series of systems and doctrines (some of them are identified with or complementary to the dogmas of the churches). They have all the same characteristic: there is no place in them for the whole man.

Unless man can be considered as the centre, in whom both matter and the spirit meet, our speculations are bound to be distorted. Any philosophy based exclusively upon science, or accounting for the world in its aspect as an object without relation to the perceiving mind and the sentient spirit, can only create a lifeless theory with some likelihood but no truth, representing an essentially indifferent world, not the world in which we are engaged.

I am not trying to build a system in which the spirit would have its due place, as I am persuaded that systems, dogmas and doctrines can only maim the exercise of free thought. To build a system for the spirit is to put a bird in a cage, drawing intellectual distinctions where there are no limits and applying general methods to the uniqueness of human experience.

My aim is rather to point out that, whatever matter may be, we find it through an expression of our faculties. If we apply this remark to literature, which is primarily expression, we have a good chance of finding that a philosophy of the spirit is implied and, as it were, embodied in it, as well as a philosophy—more explicit—of nature, life and society, a *Weltanschauung*.

It should be noted also that the philosophy of the spirit is at least as important as the philosophy of nature, for how and why we think and feel is as significant as what we think and feel about. This means that we have to swim against a powerful and massive current that invariably leads men and thoughts in one direction: the outside, as if the purpose of life were a deification of the world and a corresponding annihilation of man. Is it not the menacing trend of a civilization in which man is at best only valued as an agent for the transformation of nature and as a recipient of commodities, always in his relations to the outside, to the practical, to the surface of reality? It is a truism to say that our power over nature is gaining ground, while our power over ourselves is diminishing, and woe to the vanquished! The spirit is on the losing side, and we are frightened by the uncontrollable force of evil.

Material progress, however, has no intrinsic value, and depends entirely on spiritual progress, not exclusively on scientific acquisitions.

A philosophy and a criticism of literature has to deal with spiritual, 'unexisting' values, as opposed to objectifiable, limited facts, and inevitably ends in a unified, non-historical conception of literature, in which the literary effort is conceived as a striving for a control over the emotions and as a harmonious assimilation of experience.

At the beginning of this chapter I have shown both sides of fictitious reality : the type or character, the universal emotion shared by the reader or the audience, and the meaning of an image, a plot, a scenery or a character, the spiritual interpretation of the objective world.

Both T. S. Eliot and Benedetto Croce insist on a distinction between 'ordinary' feeling or experience and 'artistic' emotion or representation. For Croce, the difference is that 'ordinary' feeling is finite, whereas 'artistic' feeling is infinite, cannot be divided but can be shared. This theory suggests that the barriers of individual experience are transcended in art.

The same applies to ideas. In my book on modern English poetry.[2] I have been forced to draw a distinction between philosophical and poetical ideas, the former endowed with a logical, the latter with an artistic value.

I. A. Richards also shows that words cannot be taken separately, but always pre-suppose the whole :[3] "The traditional Usage Doctrine, I said, treated language on the bad

---

[2] *Thought in Twentieth Century English Poetry,* London, Routledge and Kegan Paul, Ltd., 1951.

[3] *The Philosophy of Rhetoric,* O.U.P. 1936, p. 69.

analogy of a mosaic . . ." Such a remark suggests that, apart from their logical or descriptive value, words have a value of their own.

If the existence of a literary or artistic, non-objective reality is admitted, it follows that literature is to be conceived as an emanation of the spirit, and that its essence and its value reside in the various modes of spiritual expression. The vision is what matters, not the effect or the object of the vision.

What we shall subsequently call 'vision' will mean the Logos, or the Word, life in its spiritual essence.

Although vision cannot be analysed without destroying its essential unity, it is useful to distinguish in it a series of progressive phases, which may give some notion of where it comes from and where it leads to.

Let us call objectivity or lucidity the first phase or attitude, in which the mind reduces reality to its logical elements. The final outcome of this attitude is that the objective world, divided into its finite individual elements, dissolves into nothingness and transparency. Seen from afar, the world seems meaningless and ridiculous, but we are left with the bitter lucidity of the mind : there is no escape. This is the attitude of Ecclesiastes, in which all human efforts seem vain in a vain world.

In the second phase, that of participation, the world is conceived as a whole of which the spirit is the unifying element. Instead of being divested of the spirit, the world is endowed with it until there is no separation. This is the classical attitude, for instance of Virgil's *Bucolics*. The gods are men and hide in nature.

In the third phase, that of meditation or transcendence the link with the world is again broken and the only life left to the spirit is on the successive levels of waiting, impatience, despairing, indifference and renunciation. This is partly Dante's attitude.

The three phases may of course appear under a great

variety of forms, but no other net of inherent relations is possible between the three elements : the world, man and the spirit. Literature is made of variations upon this triple theme. Here 'man' does not mean the individual with his solitary fate and his 'ordinary' emotions, but the type, the model, with whom we sympathize, whose emotions and sufferings we share.

4. LITERATURE AND LIFE OR
CORRELATION AND SEPARATION

THE fate of an individual does not move us unless it is a fate shared by all individuals, as a part of the threefold vision. There is no absolute death. However sad and horrible the event may be, it does not solve anything, it is death, and death is nothing. All happenings imply death and fate, and therefore are meaningless, individual, separated.

Seneca *(Letters to Lucilius)*, Malherbe *(Stances à Du Périer sur la mort de sa fille)*, Tennyson *(In Memoriam)*, all admit that it is impossible to uproot the grief of death for the idea of nothingness and absence is unbearable because it is physical and the spirit has no part in it. But, as soon as grief is expressed and communicated, it becomes universal and spiritual, it is transcended.

Common people, even poets, often say that they cannot express their grief or describe a beautiful thing; it is because their emotions are crude and without significance, however violent and true they may be. They are individual, closed experience. We are the 'monads without windows' of Leibnitz or Bradley's prison. We rejoice while the beggars knock at our door.

From Montaigne through Rousseau to the existentialists, from Saint Augustine to Kierkegaard, the problem of individual existence has troubled writers. None has yet been able to solve it, although all find an escape, Montaigne wisely writing that *"Tout homme porte en soi la forme entière de*

27

l'humaine condition", Rousseau telling his life, Kierkegaard in the works of love[1], the existentialists in their problematic freedom.[2] There is no solution, for the fact of the limited duration and scope of life remains. There is a certain exaltation in social life and in the national feeling, so that at 'national funerals' there is some joy in the grief shared in common. Death remains, however, a crude event, a fact before which we are powerless, and we know that any spiritual consolation is vain.

On the level of literature, however, there are no crude facts, even in the works of the naturalists, for why describe the workers' condition (as in Zola's *Germinal*), if not to arouse a certain feeling? When Dostoievski or Balzac describes a house, he sees a relation between the house and the inhabitant. The smallest detail of the closest description hides some purpose or meaning. Yes, life is very different from literature: when someone dies, he is alone, and there is no relation between his death and the colour of the tiles of his roof.

I am not suggesting that charity or socialism, medicine, work or technical advance cannot help us and diminish our isolation and our sufferings. Ideas, doctrines and practical means—all with a spiritual origin—have some influence on life and can help to make life more agreeable, joyful, peaceful and free, in other words, to add spiritual elements to it, but life remains fundamentally crude, that is, selfish, uninteresting, isolated, incommunicable. Life is limited by time, place, fate and death, and the Ancient, whose imagination was full of gods, saw very well that limitations are no gods; only the tyrannical mind of the determinists is prone to attribute a spiritual value to limitations and, smugly enough, to itself. Limits, barriers, borders, are fate, and not even the gods can change fate. Man is alone, and his dialogue is with deaf fate; your friends cannot help.

Yes, life in itself, and all things that *exist* are pointless,

[1] See the book under that title: O.U.P., London, 1946.
[2] Sartre's *Chemins de la Liberté*.

valueless, unimportant and vain. This is the cold truth, the crude and joyless reality, the immediate experience. No doctrine, no god, no technique and no policy will ever change anything about it. Because things have a beginning and an end, there is nothing but separation and existence, and separate existence is already death. We are dead and the spirit, which is life, is in us. Here I might also be accused of despising individual, 'crude' life, and of paying a compliment to the totalitarian régimes which, because they apply a doctrine or an abstract theory, are bound to destroy privacy—an aspect of what we call freedom—and so they consider man—and his spirit—only in his relations to the régime, its doctrine and its politics.

I despise the private history of both individuals and states, and I have very little confidence in established systems, doctrines and régimes, which add to the *insoluble* problem of individual life the stifling, over-burdening and inhuman problems of the powerful state and of the established church. Systems and régimes are rigid. Like our limited, particular, individual life, they consist in dead spirit. When the spirit is dead, the devil is rich.

Why am I then interested in myself, my profession and my country? This is my problem, with which theories and other people should not interfere. Individual life is to be respected because it gives birth to the spirit. The spirit is free, whereas individual life is limited, and it is the lethal aspect of life that awakens, and provokes the response of, the spirit. Anybody intensely suffering from the opaqueness of things and the isolation of existence longs for the spirit that creates the world, for the life which is the beginning and the end.

Thus real life is the beginning and the end, but our life staggers between the two. Our life is but the surface and the outcome, the result and the dead end of real life. We are dimly aware of real life, and we escape in business, practical or professional activities, physical exercise, blind belief in dogmas, adventures, love, sports, hobbies, etc., we are none the less pursued by a living reproach, for the spirit is in us and works alone if we leave it.

The escapists are not those writers who build in ivory tower and refrain from dealing with social, economic or political problems; they are those who delve into purely technical or practical problems, without caring for the spiritual implications of their work. These men are unbalanced, these writers are illiterate, but they are revered because they bring palpable results and material facts. Croce is not the only one who observes that art is not, and should not be, practical. Balzac is a great writer, not because, as Marx suggests,[3] he drew a picture of the society of his time, but because he drew it with spiritual insight.

It is not the task of the writer to meddle in social, economic or political problems, and if he does so he has to give something more than research work and practical solutions, for his solution is to be found not in the facts, but in the spirit. The whole of history, and the social, economic and political problems in it, is indirectly the product of ideas and spiritual struggles.[4] There is no escape: we are pursued, preceded, waited for and surrounded by the spirit. The solution of great problems of thought, knowledge and action does not lie in practical means, for practical means serve a finite, limited goal; it lies rather in the life of the spirit, in real life, which can be expressed by few, shared by and communicated to all.

As we have seen, there is no escape, for the whole of society as well as for the individual, there is no escape from wholeness into specialization, from values into facts, from imagination into plain common sense. The problems of the writer are not those of the psychologist, the sociologist, the economist or the politician, each of whom deals with a vast but finite field of

[3] See: Karl Marx—Friedrich Engels. *Ueber Kunst and Literatur.* Behrendt Verlag, Zürich, 1937, pp. 53, 200, 208, 214.
[4] Cf. A. N. Whitehead's *Science and the Modern World.*

'crude reality'. The writer's problems are essentially without limits. Each part of the work calls for the whole, each detail has an infinite value or is typical or is universally felt. This does not exclude precision of statement, strict delineation or even limitation of purpose. The last is traditionally indicated at the beginning of the greatest of epic poems:

> *Arma virumque cano . . .*

A long poem about drums would fail to attract universal attention. Aeneas is much more than a soldier, a *miles gloriosus,* and something else than a symbol; he is in any case no real, particular man : he is endowed with the same kind of universality as the soldier in Stephen Crane's *The Red Badge of Courage,* where we are fascinated by something more than a psychology of fear.

The writer is not responsible for particular men, but for the integrity and the wholeness of his characters. The burning of Troy, the storm on the Mediterranean, the meeting with, and the parting from, Dido, and the Latin landscapes, are component parts of Aeneas. The story has an end, but it keeps working in the mind. What attracts us in its episodes is their resonance, just as what fascinates us in Leonardo Da Vinci's early pictures is *lo sfumato,* the undefinable element of in-determination. The Gioconda's smile continues to puzzle us, because we know there is something eternal in it, as there is in the faint smile of Greek statues.

The writer has to rouse this sense of infinitude, for without it he fails to capture us. We want to be taken in, that is, to be freed from contingencies. Have you ever been "lost in a novel"? If so, you have departed for once from this world.

It is not the intellect alone that wants freedom; it is the whole man who finds this limited life and this limited world too narrow for him. Literature lies in so far as it places our life and our problems on another level and in another atmosphere than that of everyday life.[5] The trouble is that only the very great writers give us a sense of plenitude, a world in which we can breathe. The others do not lead us far enough, and we are left with complexities and limitations; life is sad and quickly forgotten. Does that explain why realism in literature stresses the ugly side of life, bare existence? Existence is separation, torment, nothingness, frustration, unrealization and illusion. The awareness of ugliness and evil is the philosophical basis of literature, ugliness and evil confronted with the sentient man. When we say that "the poetry is in the pity", we postulate the consciousness of existence, but when we accept a fixed doctrine or 'create' an objective world, we cut truth in two, remain on the level of existence, are inhuman.

The most powerful of fixed doctrines are those whose basis is a matter of belief: they cannot be proved and they are therefore forced upon believers the more tyranically and unflinchingly, regardless of human sacrifices. They are inhuman, because belief, which is a natural need, means experiment, comparison and change. Abstract, absurd, inhuman (supernatural) rites and beliefs rule individual men and nations, counteracted only by uncontrolled, unaccountable events, and we are crushed between the two blind forces, blind belief and indifference, fanaticism and cynicism; in spite of rare efforts towards harmony, moderation and unity.

It is not my purpose to judge literature by moral criteria; I only want to stress the writer's unique responsibility of guiding life—which is meaningless—towards a meaning, of transforming life—which is crude—into a spiritual experience, of transfiguring life—which is ugly—into a vision of beauty, so that the supreme interest of life lies apart from life, in real life, not in a description of every day, but in discovery and creation. Art is the only world in which we live or can live: the rest is suffering and boredom, change and forgetfulness, bestiality and blindness.

---

[5] Cf. Wordsworth's definition of poetry as "emotion recollected in tranquillity."

In a world of opposed materialisms and of closed systems, literature withdraws into criticism, and questions the values of society. We have had a literature of disgust (Sartre's *Le Mur, La Nausée, Les Mouches,* etc., Camus' *L'Etranger, La Peste,* etc.) and anarchy. The writer's responsibility seems to be satisfied with such questioning: *"il faut tout remettre en question",* and literature is revolutionary.

In a more stable period of history, the writer will be more moderate in his attacks, and his art will be a hieratic adornment of the existing state of things; I have in mind the classical periods of Greece, Rome and France. Literature is then partly official and decorative.

This broad generalization is only a superficial account of the relations between life and literature. In both types of period the responsibility of the writer is directed to the same end.

In the age of scientific revolution, in the nineteenth century, we find such apparently contradictory schools as neo-classicism (André Chénier, the Pre-Raphaelites), romanticism (a vast international movement mingling crude feelings and scientific ideas with poetry), naturalism and realism (crude facts introduced into the novel) and art for art's sake (Gautier, Mallarmé, Oscar Wilde), and of course individual geniuses such as Rimbaud.

All these types of writers are confronted with the same problem—their responsibility—and though they try to solve it in widely different ways, they all react against change and forgetfulness, suffering and boredom, bestiality and blindness. They either face the facts or embellish them; like the classics and the revolutionaries they cannot escape their conscience, and we criticize them according to their congeniality to our natures and the strength of their spirit, not according to their truth to nature. Their work is either lifeless or true, empty or beautiful, dry or fruitful. In none of them does reality consist in facts, action or techniques. Reality dwells in the work, in its wholeness, and the writer's responsibility is to place it there,

C

to answer the reader's need for unity and awareness, to ins
some plenitude and some freedom into the life of individua
and peoples.

In the preceding chapter (Life and Literature) I came to the
conclusion that the usual distinction between periods, schools
—Croce would add 'genres'—are unsatisfactory, as is my
classification, and that the unity is what matters.

The great variety of literary expression makes it clear, however, that unity is always aimed at, but never reached. The
great works are those that offer a great variety within their
unity: *Don Quixote* for example. However great a work may
be, it cannot fill the chasm between reality and literature, facts
and ideas, crude life and real life. Perfection could be attained
only in a work in which this chasm would disappear. There
subsists a discontinuity between, on the one hand, human
behaviour, the phenomena and laws of nature, and the action
or the laws of the spirit on the other hand. Kant's philosophy
ends by distinguishing two principles: moral laws and the
laws of the universe. We may suppose that they are one and
the same thing, indeed this is the safest and the most useful
hypothesis to adopt, but we cannot prove them identical, nor
can we satisfactorily join the two sides in any work of art.
The substance of our thoughts, perceptions and feelings is for
ever distinct from the substance of things. Human thought
penetrates the rocks and dissolves them a little in its acids, but
it never wholly assimilates them. As we are not satisfied with
our attempts, we imagine a divine thought which is at the
same time the force or the substance or the cause or the principle of nature, either immanent or transcendent. Again these
are philosophical distinctions with which we are not concerned. It is enough for me to suggest that the whole of litera-

35

ture is an effort towards assimilation or identification, tha
is always a partial failure and that has to be repeatedly und
taken under various forms. The distinction between nat
and the spirit subsists, and we have to build a bridge from
one to the other, unless we are torn into two pieces : the br
and the angel (Pascal).

Literary creation is to be regarded, from our point of vie
as a tension between two poles : the reality (or the substan
of things or behind things, whatever it may be, and the real
(or the essence) of thought, perception, feeling. The obj
and the subject. There is no unity and, as we have seen,
literature, if the poles are separated from each other; the
is no perfection if these opposed realities are not identical
identified. Our whole life would be impossible if the re
nature of things contradicted our perceptions, because
would have either to destroy any spiritual longings in order
dedicate ourselves to practical activities—even sleep would
forbidden, for dreams would destroy our integrity—or e
we would have to live in contemplation without eating. It
curious and refreshing to consider as an absurd hypothe
what most people are unconsciously doing. I have met ma
people in this country (Switzerland) who tell me that th
never dream and who laugh at spiritual yearnings. They w
tell you that there is no other reality than the reality of thing
The opposite type of people, equally unbalanced, is less ra
than we think; their untrained mind will lead them, with lit
resistance to excesses of blind belief, absolute rejection
evidence and negation of facts. Indeed, each of us has som
thing of both tendencies.

Fortunately we have a language which, in a precario
way, holds both poles together. Language is a creation of tw
faced symbols. Any symbol that does not represent at th
same time a thing and a thought is incomplete. The perfe
work—and literature as a whole points to this ideal—wou
bring the two poles together, would achieve identificatio
The tension is so acute and the attempt is so vast, that it h

to be repeated in various ways and under many forms. As we have seen, all writers create a reality belonging neither to things nor to thought, a double or intermediate reality that achieves more or less perfectly the identification of things and thoughts.

Sometimes, contrast is shown instead of identification. It does not matter, for the result is the same : to bring things and thought together.

A paradox is a good example of contrast. When Oscar Wilde maintains that nature imitates art, we are shocked, amused and enriched, because we see the eternal contrast of things and thought in a new light. The paradox consists in reversing the usual trend of thoughts (from the thing to the idea).

We need not choose difficult examples. Wit is another instance. When you laugh about sad things (telling them in a funny way) your spirit is at variance with facts, but this does not matter : they are brought together. There is a meeting point. Life is a perpetual occasion for such a meeting, for the simple reason that we are in constant touch with things, and endowed with a constantly reacting spirit. But things and moods can never know each other, even when they seem to agree. When this meeting is manifested in words, when moods are conscious of things, a work of literature is born. When words deal exclusively either with things or ideas, then we have something else than literature—science or religion for example. A writer may be scientific, but with a certain mood; he may deal with pure theology, but in images. In both cases the subject-matter must be moulded in an adequate form, in both cases there must be some sort of interaction or fusion within the double meaning of each symbol.

The ambivalence of literature has never been sufficiently noticed. Criticism generally destroys the integrity of works, showing one side only : either the *Weltanschauung* or the temper, either the ideas or the style. It is vaguely recognized that the style must conform to the contents, but why and how this is done is a matter of taste. Criticism is mainly an analysis either of the way of saying (temper, style), or of what is said (subject-matter, ideas, *Weltanschauung*), whereas the essence of literature is the meeting of both.

Here again we see the difference between life and literature. Life is a continuous occasion for a meeting which we always postpone because we are too busy either with our souls or with our practical purposes. We want to be saved and to win our bread, sometimes we want only bread, sometimes bread and pleasure: we always dissociate spirit and matter, the things we are in touch with, and the senses, the mind, the soul.

Let us suppose that you are walking in a street. You are shopping, or going to work. Your purpose is definite, you have to follow a certain direction on the pavement and to avoid hurting people. Whether you feel happy or unhappy has nothing to do with your purpose. You pass a blind man, but you need do nothing about it. You are in front of the building of an insurance company; its design is made of straight lines; there is no imagination and no style in it, it has nothing to do there, but it is practical, as is your purpose. You are a self-contained individual with your own purposes.

Now you are on holiday in the country. Yesterday it was raining and you could not help being a little sad about it. Today it is warm and sunny, the air is trembling, you feel exalted. You have opened your soul a little, and you know that there is a relation between the rain and your sadness, the sun and your cheerfulness, but you leave it at that, mere co-existence of nature and man.

But if you had laughed at the rain, at your damp clothes, at your silly idea of going out, nature perhaps and your mind would have met in a sparkle of wit.

People believe that certain things are sad because they are usually associated with sadness. The suffering and the joy are in yourself. In literature, however, though not in life, things and moods meet, in contrast or in union, and provoke a sparkle.

Poetry is nothing less than a miracle, for it often happens in it that one thing evokes another, or that man finds his image in nature. Facts never call to one another, and nature is inhuman. As to Vigny, the poet who complains that nature is inhuman, a stoic attitude provides him with the harmony without which there is no poetry.

Facts would be facts and the spirit would be a gratuitous phantasy in a gratuitous world, in which we had no share of responsibility, in other words in Eden, in the world preceding evil (of Baudelaire's *La Vie Antérieure*).

The fallacy of taking things in themselves leads to two opposite extremes : positivism and absolutism. Two main elements are contained in positivism : a belief in facts and a complete disregard of spiritual values. Absolutism is the contrary, that is, the belief in the absolute and exclusive value and reality of the spirit (as in Eliot's *Four Quartets*), and a corresponding contempt for the temporal world (except in so far as the latter is a toy for the established spiritual authority). Both attitudes are important and partial, both fail to see that the relation between what they adore or despise and their love or indifference is more important than either things in themselves or the absolute spirit. Both attitudes are fictitious, tyrannical creations of man's lack of balance.

The core of intolerance and meanness lies in this belief in the absolute character of distinctions. A clever man is able to draw subtle and clear distinctions, but a more intelligent man knows that those distinctions have a merely pragmatic function. The comprehensive philosophy I am trying to work out (not to establish, for fixed thought is dead thought) refrains from attributing any definite character either to the physical universe or to the spirit. The universe is what you think it is, and the spirit hides in things, so that if you attack the world too much you may injure the spirit.

Every poet recognizes the sacred spirit hidden in things, and the clever man looks down upon the poet who disregards distinctions, for the clever man knows that a tree is a tree, and the wind is not a sigh. The magic achievement of poetry, the power of phantasy, is not a discovery of the spirit, but the creation of a state or an image in which physical and spiritual elements appear in their proper unsuspected relation.

As to truth in philosophy, it should be simply a study of this correlation, instead of a contemplation of eternal, abstract values or the creation and explanation of an objective, concrete, opaque, physical universe. In a balanced philosophy the study of the human mind should be complemented by the observation of the physical universe, in order to show their similitude and their interaction. The study of their meeting points in literature would have an important place in such a philosophy.

6. THE WRITER'S RESPONSIBILITY

WE know that we and the world are evil, and although we have a tendency to confuse evil with immorality, we are also dimly aware that, as one single community and as individuals, we share some part of responsibility for this world.

We also generally accept the connection proposed by the Bible between evil and knowledge. The origin of evil is the knowledge of good and evil. We are less sure about the nature of evil. We are satisfied with saying that evil means disobedience to the laws of God, but the ten commandments reveal nothing of its nature. It was an easy solution to attribute evil to the demons; then, with the Reformation, evil consisted in being deaf to the voice of conscience; but what is conscience? Is it not a sense of unity, the longed-for ideal identification of the spirit with the world?

If we accept this suggestion, we realize that we live in a permanent state of evil, for the exclusive pursuit of practical ends or of spiritual satisfactions and, more generally, any activity implying a dichotomy of the world and the spirit, would be evil.

We are at present fearing—and witnessing—an evil use of atomic and economic powers. Is it not characteristic of a practical device, based upon objective research, being used in complete disregard of spiritual, non-objective demands? Is not the most dangerous form of vice a desire for possession, rather than a pursuit of pleasure? The pursuit of pleasure is much less dangerous because it remains primarily individual. But possession is revered as a sign of strength; we adore power, and power is evil.

Should you argue that possession is neutral, that what is evil is a bad use of possession, I would say that possession has been reached through evil. Of course I cannot admit that the possession of a roof and a loaf of bread is evil, because those are within our essential needs. Possession, which involves the creation of an outside, independent reality, is evil, the root of which is 'pure' objectivity, or the knowledge of reality.

The same might be said of the knowledge of the spirit, that is, purely theoretical knowledge, in complete disregard of facts. This is not the place for describing the evil consequences of abstract systems and their corresponding fanaticism.

Besides, the two extremes are intimately connected. Today we see that the theory of objectivity, which is a construction of the mind, leads to a consecration of the facts, from which the mind is absent. Dispossession leads to possession, and no good is to be expected from facts.

My main point in this discussion is that facts are neither neutral nor beautiful, which is the same thing for my next point is that beauty is neutral.

Beauty may contain a portraiture of evil, but is neutral in itself. I am not going to give a definition of beauty, but it is convenient to remember here that Plato considered it as an idea. Is not beauty a relation between a thing and an idea, is not a beautiful thing one that conforms to certain ideal standards of our mind and senses? The essence of beauty also, in literature and elsewhere, resides in ambivalence, in the meeting between things and ideas and beauty as such does not belong to this world. It is either neutral or good, for it is either a response or an act of responsibility.

Nothing is beautiful in itself; the same thing may seem beautiful to some, ugly to others. Beauty seems : good *is*. A thing is good in itself; whether it seems so or not does not matter, because it proceeds from a good act. A good act is an act of responsibility towards other beings, a beautiful thing is a natural thing that provokes a response (in this case neither the thing nor its admirer have any merit) or a work of art proceeding from an act of responsibility and constituting a bridge between facts and the spirit (in this case merit lies not with the admirer who recognizes the ambivalence, but with the author who has created it).

All this may seem, of course, over-simplified, dogmatic and heretical. For the members of a Church it is safer to accept that evil is disobedience to God, without commenting upon it, or asking what it means.

The only discovery I claim is my suggestion that evil implies a dichotomy of the whole man, a separation of the spirit from nature, either a doctrinal disregard for facts or a materialistic pursuit. The rest follows, so that from these premises I must be judged.

The failure of abstract morality and the impossibility of realism (meaning here any knowledge or action derived exclusively from facts) confirm my conception of truth, beauty and good, as a meeting of two confluent streams, and of ideal inexistence in both consciousness and nature as the principle and end of both existence and facts, so that it is as impossible for ideas to change the course of events as it is for facts to alter ideas. The flux of events dissolves into unchangeable unity, in which all our limited desires, emotions, aspirations, feelings and conceptions end. There is no end, no peace, no rest, no meeting in this life. That is why men have felt it necessary to create in literature a fictitious reality that will constitute a meeting point for ideas and facts, a place of rest and infinite resonance, where events have a meaning because consciousness has an influence.

Our distinction between the subjective and the objective, between moral and natural laws, ideas and facts, the spirit and matter (the list of parallel dualities could be prolonged) is quite artificial. Kant and Emerson, among others, have been led to taking these distinctions of the mind for a dichotomy of reality. The universe and the spirit seem to constitute two separate entities, but I have good reasons for supposing that they *are* identical. The words 'spirit' and 'things' are symbols for two aspects of the same reality. Reality is one, but the human mind divides it in two: appearances and existence, facts and will.

A scientific study of a bird, with all the technical means of observation, and a complete accumulation of the facts about it, will not give you the slightest hint of the real bird unless you interpret the facts and have some insight into the bird's being, existence and behaviour. Reality is facts plus understanding, knowledge plus experience, an apparent and relative ambivalence which suggests the final oneness of reality and the falsity of one-sided views or actions. If we accept this conception of the wholeness of reality, the problems of knowledge, time and evil appear in a new light, and we understand the ambivalent reality of literature better.

Any sound criticism of literature must at the same time be a criticism of life. Croce maintains that Tasso's allegory in his *Jerusalem,* a product of the Counter-Reformation, is of historical interest, but is not artistic, so that an appreciation of its value implies a philosophy of history[1] as well as æsthetic judgment. Both classicism *(critica estetica)* and historicism *(critica storica)* are crippled by their common hatred of philosophy *(hanno in comune l'odio contro la filosofia in genere e contro il concetto dell'arte in ispecie:)*. Any philosophy of literature will therefore involve at the same time a criticism of life, a speculative philosophy and an æsthetics.

Croce ascribes a reality to art, the reality of intuitions within the unity of the spirit, but his whole philosophy—and his philosophy of art—is based upon the assumption that reality is the spirit, not, as I suggest, the identity of spirit and things, a continuously creative and modified relation or, in literature, the co-existence of observation and intuition and, in poetry, their harmony.

In order to show the essential difference between the

[1] Breviario di Estetica, Bari, Laterza, 1913, p. 123.

æsthetics I propose and Croce's, I quote a passage in which, (after criticizing Vico, Kant und Hegel for considering history as rational, so that events are but shadows and products of the spirit) Croce propounds his own view of history, not as the end-product of concepts, but as the changing, multiple and individual aspect of the absolute : *"Se si domanda, delle varie attivita dello spirito, quale sia reale, o se siano tutte reali, bisogna rispondere che nessuna è reale; perchè reale è solamente l'attività di tutte quelle attività, che non riposa in nessuna di esse in particolare: delle varie sintesi, che abbiamo via via distinte—sintesi estetica, sintesi logica, sintesti practica, —sola reale è la sintesi delle sintesi, lo Spirito, che è il vero Assoluto, l'actus purus. Ma, per un altro verso e per la stessa ragione, utte sono reali, nell' uni tì dello spirito, nell' eterno corso e ricorso, che è la loro eterna costanza e realtà. Coloro che nell'arte vedevano o vedono il concetto, la storia, la matematica, il tipo, la moralità, il piacere, e ogni altra cosa, hanno ragione, perchè in essa, in forza dell' unità dello spirito, sono queste e tutte le altre cose."*[2]

The difference is at the same time an important and a subtle one. According to Croce, both things and perceptions, facts and thoughts, are particular manifestations of the absolute spirit. Croce overlooks the fact that there are two ways which end in the spirit : the way beginning with facts and the way beginning with intuitions, the material and the spiritual way, which we have been led to conceive as converging ways which end in identity. All philosophers have tried in many ways to reduce or to dismiss the discrepancy, at the level of brute life and individual existence, between things and thoughts. None of these attempts can be satisfactory, for human existence is an apparently absurd co-existence of the things perceived or unknown and the perceiving or ignorant soul. Any attempt at uniting these two elements on the level of existence is bound to fail. The existentialists are right in pointing out that existence is absurd, be-

[2] op. cit., p. 89, 90.

cause there is no logic, no unity, no coherence in it; it is continuously unfulfilled and unreal : reality and unity are to be found on another level, and here I think Croce would agree. As soon as we find a reaction, a meaning or a link, we are outside existence, in reality.

Existence is the co-existence of unsentient things—the universe—with consciousness—the sentient, pleasure-seeking and suffering mind and soul—that seeks a realization, a meeting with things without which the soul is unreal. Living thought is the soul in action, deciphering what, in the world, is consubstantial with the spirit. For what can we understand and feel, if not that which is made of the same substance as our soul?

Knowing that the core of any great philosophy is truth, that is, living thought, I do not wish to refute Croce or others. I only want to insist on the points that distinguish my views on life or literature from those of philosophers or art critics.

A philosopher asks what are nature, life, the essence, the substance, the spirit, an idea, or concrete things, good and evil, fate, chance or the free will, and then asks why and to what purpose these things exist. He rarely inquires at the same time into the nature of what we see, or do not see, feel, perceive and conceive, on the one hand, and of our vision, feeling, perception and conception or ignorance on the other hand. Things in themselves are merely hypotheses or projections of our mind, so that the most realistic, positive and objective of philosophies can end only in imagining an artificial universe, not the one in which we live, with which we co-exist and outside of which we cannot think.

Similarly, the most spiritual, idealistic and transcendental of philosophies can end only in a complete disregard of the basic facts of life.

The same thing happens to those critics whose method is based either upon historical research or upon æsthetic principles : they also concern themselves exclusively with facts or canons in themselves, separately or successively conceived, never together and essentially united, even if it is in an explosive mixture. They introduce a distinction into a reality (literature) which is real because it is a union of two varieties of correlative elements. Considering each of the two elements in itself, they are left with something else than literature.

The characteristic of the present philosophy of literature is that I am not interested in finding out whether things are this or that, whether an author states or believes or feels this or that, and how, why, when or where he does so. My concern is with the doubleness, togetherness, meeting, repulsion or connection in literature, of that which is separated, co-existent and confronted in life. I am not asking whether things are so or otherwise, I am asking what things are felt, are thought, are perceived, are conceived, are imagined. The purpose of my philosophy of literature is to explore into the convergence of the spirit and nature in the works in which their unity is realized. The following geometrical diagram may serve to illustrate this purpose: (see p. 48.)

Having thus defined my purpose in abstract terms, I have now to consider the concrete side of the present philosophy of literature, which I call concrete and real is so far as it unites the spirit and nature.

Practical criticism is not my aim, for that would imply an evaluation of one or several works. My aim is to study the possibilities of literary expression, and, so far as these possibilities are realized in existing works, this will entail some practical criticism.

For example, if I study an author's ideas, I consider them as the expression of a certain temperament combined with the result of certain observations. I do not consider separately what he says and how he says it, I study a strange, double reality in which the author's existence and the existence of things unite. A possibility is realized through the expression of these ideas in words. I am not concerned with the truth of these ideas, their confirmation through events or with the

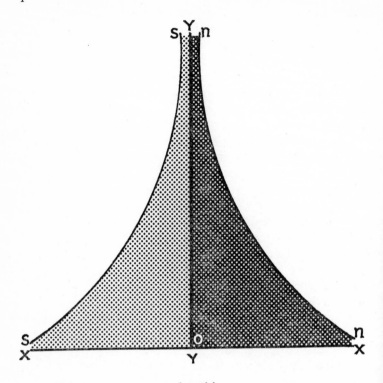

the curve s   represents the spirit
the curve n   represents nature
the asymptote x   represents existence; s and n come nearer to
                   existence in proportion as they diverge from
                   each other: it is the surface of life
the asymptote y   represents art, in which s and n are brought
                   together; the deeper (or higher) art is,
                   the closer s and n are, and the farther x is.
                   The purpose is to follow y from the centre o,
                   not to the ideal point where s and n meet, but
                   to the point where y ceases to be finite, for art
                   has human dimensions
          In the drawing s and n exist separately in relation to x, but they
exist together in relation to y.

adequacy of the form in which they appear : these three kinds of investigation are the task of the critics. I am concerned with the concrete realization of an ideal possibility, with a solution of a problem or the convergence of complexities.

The whole conception of life, objectivity, evil and reality, as expounded in the preceding chapters, is pre-supposed in the following applications. I do not proceed from a pre-conceived system or from a particular point of view, I study the whole-ness and reality of literary expression, as it appears in a few chosen instances and as it is possible. I am only building a method, hoping others will apply it successfully and improve it.

It may be objected that Croce, too, insists on the unity of art and criticizes the misleading distinctions[3] of form and con-tents, intuition and expression, fantasy and technique, bare and ornate expression. I admit these considerations, but I must reject his conclusion :[4] art is not unilaterally intuition, but intuition plus physical existence. Croce is always about to pass the border and to conceive art as a unity of that which co-exists in brute life, but the following final quotation shows where the difference lies : for Croce, art is self-sufficient and implies a negation of the physical world, not, as I maintain, an assimilation of it or a meeting with it : *"L'arte, intesa como intuizione, secondo il concetto che ho esposto, avendo negato di fronte a sè un mondo fisico, e consideratolo come una semplice costruzione del nostro intelletto, non sa che cosa farsi del parallelismo della sostanza cogitante e della sostanza estesa, e non ha da promuovere impossibili matrimoni, perchè la sua sostanza cogitante, o, per meglio dire, il suo atto intuitivo è perfetto in sè, ed è quel fatto medesimo che l'intelletto cos-truisce poi come esteso."*[5]

There is no doubt, after this quotation, that art, or intuition, is "conceiving substance", independent from, and excluding

[3] op. cit., II, Pregiudizi intorno all'arte.
[4] "l'arte rimane perfettamente definita, quando semplicemente si definisce como intuizione." op. cit. p. 45.
[5] op. cit., p. 57.

D

"existing substance", and not, as the fundamental argume
of this book suggests, a meeting of both substances. Croce
certainly one of the few philosophers who really understar
poetry; I do not question the value of his books on æsthetic
but I am compelled to observe that his concept of reality
incomplete, for his concepts both of the absolute spirit and
intuition are deprived of their correlative realization in wh
he calls the physical universe. They are considered in them
selves, as self-sufficient, abstracted from their necessary accom
paniment of facts, things, events and natural laws, which a
in turn nothing in themselves.

Croce's error consists in considering intuition as sel
sufficient. We need a wider conception of art and of reality
we want to build up a philosophy of literature which includ
all the possible forms of literary expression in its scope. Othe
wise we are forced to exclude the study of some valuab
works because they would transcend our categories. I suppo
that a large number of historical works, novels, short storie
travel books, etc., some of which are real works of art, woul
hardly conform to Croce's definition of 'intuition' as implyin
a negation of the physical universe.

There is a similar notion of works of art being created b
themselves and reacting upon one another, as if the physica
universe did not exist, in Malraux' *Philosophie de l'Art*.

7. THE COMPLETE REALITY

I CANNOT help comparing my theory—of reality as relation—with Unamuno's theory of reality as point of view. I choose Unamuno because, like Croce, he comes very near to my views, so that I have to take my stand on his behalf, in order to see where he can be helpful and where I differ, where I stand.

According to Unamuno, we have four 'positions' or attitudes; two are positive : to want to be and to want not to be; two are negative : not to want to be and not to want not to be.[1] Most people, or the 'crepuscular' common people, are satisfied with the negative attitudes, but real people and, among them, the heroes of good novels, either want to be or want not to be.

All these distinctions imply a conception of reality as creation, faith, will or ideal. For Don Quixote the reality was never constituted by the windmills, but by the giants. Faith is the source of reality, because it is life. To believe is to create *("Creer es crear")*.

Reality is just the bare soul or the bare will of characters, and the accumulation of details in Balzac has no other purpose than to lay bare the souls of his characters. Balzac did not lose time in observation : he carried the world within himself.

---

[1] "Hay, en efecto, cuatro posiciones, que son dos positivas: (a) querer ser; (b) querer no ser; y dos negativas; (c) no querer ser; (d) no querer no ser."
Tres Novelas Ejemplares y un Prologo, Espasa Calpe, p. 14 (Collección austral, 1945).

All this is very ingenious and fascinating. Unamuno is very impatient with facts and with realism in the novel; he even denies facts, denies the reality of the windmills. With him, reality is what you imagine, and sometimes the creations of your imagination acquire a life of their own, as they do in Shakespeare. They live on your substance until you cease, not to be, but to be real.

Such a theory throws much light on the characters in a tragedy and, to a lesser extent, on those in the novel, but I doubt whether it accounts for all the elements of reality or literary creation. I am ready to accept that faith, will or creation is a source of reality, but is not *the* source of reality. That faith, that will, is utterly intolerant and self-sufficient, it creates with a complete disregard of facts, and, when confronted with facts—with windmills—it is not in the least altered. This passionately Spanish view of reality is what we call absolutism, or a conception of the spirit in itself. There is no balance in it, no relation between spirit and things, only a tyrannical possession of things by the spirit. Reality—what I call reality—consists in a relation between the two poles of existence, in unity, not in unilateral existence either in the world where materialism confines us or in the spiritual world where absolutism lets us starve. Unless the spirit is identified with nature or recognizes its very substance in things, we experience no more than half the truth. I agree with Unamuno when he maintains that a symbol, an asymptote, or a character may live a real life of its own, but I add that a symbol is a synthesis, the meeting of an idea (or a creation) with a fact. The asymptote is no doubt a pure, ideal geometrical figure, but it corresponds both to the needs of our thought and to the ideal, secret structure of the physical universe. We continuously invent new symbols and new characters because we are striving to recover our lost identity, to reach the reality that is broken in our divided existence. Is not this strife the fundamental impulse of *Paradise Lost,* the meaning of tragedy, and the purpose of any 'real' novel?

The characters of a novel or a play are no mere ghosts, they (to come back to Unamunos's four attitudes) are never pure will or pure faith, mere fear or mere indifference. They remain unreal until they find some concretion or incarnation in a shape, an image, an action, an actor and a voice. They are both spirit and appearance, the meeting of which is reality.

If a character has almost nothing concrete about it, as to some extent, is the case of Unamuno's novels, it remains unreal, in spite of its violent passions, and I wonder how the author or the reader can conceive it without attributing to it at least an appearance corresponding to his desires and beliefs, so that the reader my feel and see something, for he is not prepared to accept a reality which is nowhere and always (as Eliot—another absolutist—defines the impossible abstract stillness of the universe, an entity with which we have nothing to do).

Milton, who attributes an appearance to God and his angels, knew this need well. It is as indispensable for a writer to give a form to his ideas as for a scientist to interpret his observations. What we call a 'living' character is made of two elements : the spirit which is in him and moves him, and the concretion of that spirit or the obstacles to that spirit, the bodily existence suggested by the author or assumed by the actor. The readers or the audience identify themselves with the character whatever his outward appearance may be, they feel as he feels, they can sympathize with his desires because his desires are awakened in them, but the character has his own fate, in which is illustrated the struggle between human will and destiny, the identification of the spirit with destiny, nature and God. In that identification lies the reality and the meaning of both tragedy and comedy, not to speak of the novel.

The conscious or unconscious purpose of any literary work dealing with characters is to create a harmonious relation between the will of the characters and their fate, so that their life become a real unity, without which, as I have suggested, there is no work of art. The readers or the audience identify themselves with the characters, but they are different, for they live on another plane of existence. The readers or the audience cannot grasp their own life as a whole, because they live in the present; but what they see on the stage or read in the novel, the short story or the poem has a beginning and an end : they are offered the whole story, and the whole story, in art, must be an equation of two symbols, the spirit and the world, the will and what happens. The solution of the equation is what we call reality.

It is not sufficient for the author to create a character out of his own substance and to endow him with an appearance : he has to judge him, to see him as a whole, as a relation, as a reality. The character will live, not according to his will only, but according to his fate, so that it is a necessity for the author, not only to know his character, but also to know what is opposed to or modifies him. That is the whole story, the equation of fate and will, appearance and spirit, without which we are not convinced of the character's reality.

It would not be difficult to illustrate this account. The very notion of drama implies a tension, a conflict, which has to be solved by the author. When, as in Corneille's *Le Cid,* the solution does not take place within the play, we are not quite satisfied; it looks as if the author was not able to judge his characters, or did so according to non-artistic standards. In any event we are frustrated, because we do not witness the whole story. Rodrigue and Chimène live before us for some time, but they are not real. They would be real if the conflict had come to a solution, not to a compromise.

One of the most real characters in literature is Don Quixote, because he is constantly rebuked by fate, constantly firm and coherent in his purposes, although mad, although at times disturbed, and because the whole story is told with humour and pity, sympathy and irony. Not only does the author value his characters, but they judge each other, and they are judged by events. What adds to the reality of the novel and makes a masterpiece of it, is that its very theme contrasts and finally unites the two poles of faith and common sense, madness and evidence. In his *Vida de Don Quijote y Sancho Panza*[2] Unamuno gives us a living interpretation of Cervantes' great work. His re-creation of the two inseparable characters, although at times inaccurate, makes us familiar with the spiritual implications of the novel, but what Unamuno, who exploits the radiating power of concrete details, cannot re-create, is the concrete reality of the novel, and the possibility of *several* interpretations. Is it a picture of the whole of human life? Whether we interpret it as a symbol or, as the notes in the scholarly editions do, as a unique and factual account, we are startled by the unity and the simplicity of that apparently complex and uneventful story: Don Quixote and Sancho may be, as Unamuno interprets them, ideal characters: they are none the less real, that is, different from us who exist, because in them the spirit and the world are presented as one whole, with conflicting elements, but still one whole. They are developed like a theorem based upon the equation of fate and will. The fact that no character can be studied in himself, abstracted from his environment and from his fate, is illustrated, I suppose, by all novels. By environment and fate, however, I do not mean simply descriptions of nature, scenery and what happens in the novel: I allude rather to the creative attitude of the author. The character is nothing in himself, unless the author ascribes to him a certain meaning and places him within the frame of his whole conception of life. The theory of the indifferent author is factitious. The meaning of any character is inseparable from the author's attitude. According to the type of character, the author may be sympathetic or critical, but never indifferent. The theory of objective creation, and the corresponding neutral attitude of the writer, is a gross error. Objectively seen, the character may exist, but it remains unreal, for the reality of the character

[2] Espasa Calpe, Collección Austral, 1938.

consists in the coincidence of his existence with the writer's imaginative conception of it.

Sometimes the author's judgment is explicit, in Pirandello's plays for example. Sometimes it is fused in the character, for it is part of the character's reality.

It is as impossible to create characters from nothing as it is to take them from what people call 'real life'. A large proportion of university criticism consists, alas, in looking for the documents, the historical facts and the objective data, and then comparing the author's version with what the professor and the student take for reality. They do not realize that what they take for reality is merely fixed existence, that is, death, and that the creative writer has nothing to do with that kind of material. These studies are useful for students of geography, biography and history, but they mislead the student of literature, instead of focusing his interest on the writer's elaboration of facts.

The author's judgment of things, which I call reality, cannot be characterized better than by quoting some of the innumerable passages in which it appears. Let us extract a fragment from the reality of a novel by Ramuz : *"Les plantes étaient attachées par leurs racines aux poutres et pendaient, la tête en bas, comme des chauves-souris."*[3]

Here is part of a narrative :

"There came upon me, as though I had felt myself losing my footing in the midst of waters, a sudden dread, the dread of the unknown depths."[4]

Banquo's remark, after his and Macbeth's first meeting with the witches :

"The earth hath bubbles, as the water has,
And these are of them : whither are they vanish'd ?"

---

[3] *Si le Soleil ne revenait pas,* Paris, Grasset, 1939, p. 146.
[4] *Lord Jim,* by Joseph Conrad, The Albratross, 1948, p. 284.

A last quotation, from "Written by Somebody on the Window of an Inn at Stirling, on Seeing the Royal Palace in Ruin", by Burns.[5]

> "The injured Stuart line is gone,
> A race outlandish fills their throne;
> An idiot race, to honour lost;
> Who know them best despise them most."

I have quoted four very different passages dealing with what people—and some scholars—call 'unreal things' in order to illustrate my notions of unity and reality.

The bats, the fear, the witches and the dead kings are excluded from what people call 'reality', that is, from existence, they exist only in imagination, and yet they are living realities, palpable and conceivable, made from the flesh and from the spirit in such a way that it is impossible to disentagle the flesh from the spirit. That unity is a feature of art, not of existence, and we need neither examine the passages in detail nor consider their relation to the whole works: they are sufficient evidence for the importance of studying the ambivalent unity of expression rather than comparing fiction with facts.

In the study of literature the philosopher should not aim at finding out what life is or how life is presented in literature. The question is: what is real life, life that is felt, thought, experienced, acted, laughed at, rejected; not life in itself, but life that is experienced, worked-out life: reality.

The philosopher has therefore very little to say, unless he himself is a creative writer, and his task is all the more difficult because he is able to analyse concrete symbols, but he cannot make a philosophical synthesis. Artistic expression keeps the monopoly of the synthesis for which the philosopher strives.

As soon as we criticize Burns' statement for example, saying that it is a passionate, blind expression of convictions, we

[5] Poetical Works of Robert Burns, Collins, p. 28.

appeal to an ideal synthesis, to a balanced attitude resulting from a convergence of observation and belief, intuition and expression. Whatever our own convictions and experiences may be, we cannot but agree with an author who achieves that harmony.

8. THE DEFEAT OF EVIL

ART is neutral and real, but events, so far as we play some part in them, are either bad or good, and, as long as we are not conscious of them, unreal. What exists has no reality in itself, and is either bad or good. Nothing is indifferent, things are waiting for us to choose as soon as we are in touch with them, as soon indeed as we are merely aware of them.

The danger of modern science has two sides: the neutral attitude of the scientist and the neutral character with which he endows his 'object'. In the tragic development of contemporary physics, the scientist has committed himself, almost without knowing it, to evil. As an official state institution, science becomes an instrument of good or evil politics.

The fact that the best historians are not scientists in the strict sense of the word, but men of letters, warns us that it is impossible for the historian to remain neutral: he deals with human actions, and his theme can less easily be reduced to indifferent raw materials than other themes that are less obviously connected with man.

Evil plays such an important part in history that it is surprising that no history of evil has ever been written. In order to understand evil's part in history, I refer again to my definition of evil: a unilateral aim or action, pride of the spirit or desire of possession. In the light of that definition, history appears as a monstrous show of pride and possession.

Crude actions and events always mean a coexistence of spirit and things whose separation is ended in the work of art or in the historical interpretation. There is perhaps a moral power at work in history, and we may believe in some sort

59

of providence, but unless we have an historian to show us a
principle of unity, that is, of harmony between spiritual needs
and the conditions of existence, history remains a heap of evil
and dreary raw materials.

So long as mottoes like 'time is money' or 'business is business' prevail, the scientific approach to economics—which
pretends to ignore the factors of good and evil—will ignore
the basic aspect of economic life: the universal struggle between good and evil.

If evil comes from limitations and separation, it has to be
recognized as the most familiar fact of life, so familiar indeed
that we forget it. Is not existence itself, meaning limitation
and separation, evil? Is not the purpose of a good life to overcome limitation and separation, to create and to be freed from
evil, that is, from existence? If so, the triumph of evil is an
illusion, for it is a victory of meanness, blindness, bare facts
and crude events. In so far as man is neither a blind fanatic
nor an insensitive materialist, there is still a struggle against
evil. Evil triumphs in existence and in crude historical events,
but good is the complete reality, the harmony of life transcend-
ing bare existence. Human life is the meeting ground of good
and evil, of complete, ideal reality and of limited, bare existence. Unsolved, mixed, ambiguous, unstable, inconclusive, it
leads to wholeness, or falls into oblivion.

The most universal means of overcoming limitation and of
endowing existence with a meaning are belief and love.

9. BELIEF AND LOVE IN LITERATURE

BELIEF is such a powerful and constant driving force in, around or behind literature that it is possible to speak of a Buddhistic, an Islamic or a Christian literature. If the writer believes in a special God (as believers are usually exclusive, I have allowed myself this restrictive epithet; when they are not exclusive they are vague) he tries inevitably to propagate his faith. Since the purpose of his work is to communicate a belief, he bears a heavy responsibility, for he presents to millions of future readers what he alone has acquired. In the three religions mentioned, he contributes to the persistence, the fixity and the enrichment of a creed that was embodied, propagated, acted on and established more than a thousand years before. His work is a monument of make-believe, a work of propaganda.

If the writer doubts, his work will stir up the pains of doubt in his readers, and if he does not believe at all, he will still have to take his stand: if he attacks religion, his work will none the less bear so firm an imprint of the belief he has got rid of, that it is ridiculous for a Western writer to declare that he is not a Christian, or for an Arab, I suppose, that he is not a Mohammedan.

Nobody can live without any kind of belief. The power of a coherent and all-pervading faith is such that it will abide throughout many centuries, whether true or not, especially if it involves a justification of, or gives a meaning to, human suffering. For those who suffer it is difficult not to feel alone, abandoned, and it is quite natural that those who suffer much should hate God. On the whole, however, men have shown a longing to believe, so that religions have shown a tendency to establish themselves comfortably as a revered authority living on faith just as governments—monarchies, dictatorships or democracies—live on opinion. Suffering and the individual life are allowed to pass away unnoticed : the faith remains. Any faith disregards individual life : otherwise it will not survive.

Love is even more universal, for more works are inspired by love than by religion. The passion of love also makes life interesting, distracts the attention from the crude experience of existence and produces an illusion, a pleasant dream. But love has no enemies : that explains perhaps why it is more universal. Nobody objects to a love-story, provided that it is unreal enough. There are no anti-lovers, their are either indifferent writers, who fall into two categories : the cold ones and the disillusioned ones, or haters—but hate is another passion.

Christian love has inspired a few works, though rarely those dealing with charity or written in its name : I am rather thinking of works that denounce a social abuse or bravely attack a false creed. The exaltation of brotherly love is nothing but a sense of unity, that is, of reality, and has little to do with the creation, maintenance and fixation of illusions by love, of a church by belief, and of a government by opinion. Illusions, churches and governments exist upon trust. They feed upon the sublimation of sexual desire, the need to overcome ignorance, and the acceptance of authority. The more they transcend man the more they show his weaknesses. Paradoxically, they debase man all the more because he wants to escape from his animality, his ignorance and his servitude. They have few traces of spirituality, truth and freedom, but they stand for them in the eyes of brutish, ignorant slaves, who remain all the more firmly enslaved because they are unable to bring order into their lives. They read day-dreams and they make love in obscurity, they go to church and they are narrow-minded, they worship power and they care but for their own selves. It is easy to delude oneself as well as others, either by believing in absolute truth or by transfiguring life through love. Belief and love are often an escape from existence into unreality, but in rare cases, of which literature is one, they are also a liberation from unreality and a revelation of truth.

I cannot emphasize enough the accidental character of life. Anything we experience is a chance happening. Nothing can be foreseen because everything is forgotten. Whatever happens does not matter, does not change anything. The things we experience are always truncated.

We are never satisfied, and because we have a spirit living in us we should like to correct nature. We cannot refrain from intervening. Action, revolt, desire for order and unity: are not these—and not imitation—the principle of art? When an artist looks at the branches of a bare tree, either he sees some necessity, some grace, some order in their lines, or he unconsciously corrects them. The more we look at things, the more mistaken they seem. They flee from our grasp like ghosts; they are but the possibilities of becoming a meaning.

The purpose of literature and art is to seize these opportunities, to go where they point to, and not to stay *hic et nunc*, in the world of broken objects and chance meetings. There is only one danger on the way, to forget that they are nothing in themselves.

If we elaborate an absolute system, we forget that we deal with unreality; if we judge everything from a universal criterion and decide for ever what is good or bad, we lose touch with reality.

The problem of knowledge precedes the ontological problem: the answer to 'what is?' depends on the answer to 'what do we and what can we know?' When belief becomes dogmatic and love blind, we are no artists: instead of correcting nature, we ignore it.

A universal criterion would be useful if things were things, but things are what they are plus what we perceive and believe they are.

Literature is interpretation. A writer who is satisfied with factual statements is boring and uninspired, and a writer whose love and belief lack concrete foundations is a liar. The bores and the liars are much more numerous than the artists, for it is easier to collect documents or to delude oneself and convince others than to understand something.

There is a great difference between permanence, which is real, and fixation, which is death, or rather timelessness, dryness and abstraction. I was going to add 'lifelessness' to the preceding list of abstract terms, but I realized that, instead of an absence of life, fixation rather involves violence, for it is the very basis of authority and servitude, domination, hierarchy, discipline, despotism and tyranny.

In his *Agonia del Cristianismo,* Unamuno criticizes Catholicism for its being established, fixed in hierarchic forms, and Protestantism for its literal interpretation of the Word, another kind of fixation. As soon as belief crystallizes in a fixed form, it becomes fanaticism.

It is important to know as exactly as possible what an author means, but it is much more important to study what he means to us, for the purpose of literature is not to produce, multiply, order and accumulate written works: the end of literature is to keep the spirit alive. The written word, if taken literally, may become an instrument of tyranny and boredom.

Fixed—or, as I also called them, absolute—ideas are as narrow and tyrannical as limited facts (facts or events are always limited or, as I have called them, crude) and fixed institutions (laws, for example, are either imposed by violence or evaded, unless they are in accordance with the living spirit of the peoples; they never have a life of their own).

It is refreshing to note that in philology—contrary to literature—much attention has been devoted to the living word for example in the works of the Genevese school of 'stylistique' and still more, by many English scholars, for the importance of the spoken word is more obvious in English than in French

From the Introductory Chapter of H. C. Wyld's *History of Modern Colloquial English*[1], I quote the following wise statement: "If a language ceases to be spoken as a normal, living means of intercourse between man and man, the written form can no longer change, but must remain fixed, since it must consist merely of a reproduction of ancient models; there is no longer a living, changing speech to mould its character and keep it up to date."

This reminds us of the element of fixity contained in the written word and warns us that too much importance should not be attributed to the texts themselves. Documents are documents, and in themselves they serve no end.

Fanaticism and dead documents are close allies, so are also convential love and materialism. Existence can be reduced to sex and money, but life is more than that. Real love, that finds poetic expression, is as far from sin as Kierkegaard's *Works of Love* is from pornography.

As component parts of literature, love and belief create, transmit and give a meaning to life (but life is meaning) or else they merely adorn sex and mummify thought.

[1] Reprinted in 1956.

E

10. SOME APPLICATIONS

So far I have been concerned with literature as a whole, although, at times, I have applied my philosophical theory of literature to some definite elements in it, for example the characters of a play or a novel.

Any work of any kind may be examined in the same manner, provided that the philosopher avoids too rigid a classification and keeps always in mind the relation between the particular work or aspect or word and the whole of literature as living thought.

In a very simple and general way, satire, whether humorous or the fruit of indignation, is unthinkable without a consciousness of social abuses. Even if the abuses—the facts—are not commented upon by the poet, they provoke a response from the reader: they are interpreted, and what I call the ambivalence of literature is here clearly demonstrated.

I could go deeper, and interpret a satire, but I am not here concerned with analysis. I only mention that, in Greek, Roman, French and English literature, satire has complied with certain rules and has been set into a fixed form. This brings us to a consideration of *prosody*.

The essence of prosody—and the law of art—is unity. Now this unity does not exist in complex nature. Unity is an idea, a spiritual value, a law which does not exist, but has to be artificially and artistically created. Prosody is an imperfect means of producing it, not more imperfect than any other means of creating unity, or, more generally, of expressing in words the hidden spiritual universe, which is the end and the beginning of the temporal one.

It is not surprising that prosody should in its origins be linked to magic and incantation. Rhythm and repetition, rhyme and alliteration or assonance build the words into a unifying structure, place them, as it were, in a spiritual atmosphere. It is movement suggesting stillness, controlled movement or dancing.

The danger of a fixed prosody, however, is that it often provokes a distinction between form and contents, between the mould—or the ornaments—and the materials. In that event, it is better to throw away the established prosody as a dead, and cumbering object.

The great advantage of prosody is to provide a link between the ideal requisite of unity and the physical elements of language so transformed into music.

Imagine the romantic poets without rhythm! The regular, impersonal elements of rhythm and composition save them from their uninteresting (because individual) idiosyncrasies and give life to their dull narrations:

> The winds are high on Helle's wave
> (Byron, *The Bride of Abydos,* Canto II, 1)

There is little doubt, however that prosody *is* merely the instrument. Poetry admits neither the primacy of skill nor the primacy of subject-matter: either the poet expresses himself strongly, clearly and elegantly, bringing his human presence to the reader, and we say that he is skilful, or he communicates an overwhelming sense of awe or mystery, bringing unknown beauty or ungraspable reality to the reader, and we say that he is profound.

In both cases he may have nothing to say, for what is there to be said? Life is but money and sex, and you cannot be poetic about them. Besides, whether life is so or otherwise does not matter: it is what you feel that is in question. Not the feeling alone, but the presence and the feeling, the feeling of the presence and the presence of the feeling.

What the poets have to say, what they point to, what they suggest and want, desire and declare, has little importance. Whether the reader is moved or indifferent is also of secondary importance. The only important thing is what the poem *is*, if it has any reality in itself, if its words are memorable, and if, involving as it were a reality in its mood, it succeeds in closing its net on the appropriate form. A sincere poet is not a poet who expresses his feelings without a disguise, he is a poet who is able to transform a feeling or an impression into words, and sincerity is not the only requisite.

I am not going to indulge in a theory of poetic values and the poetic impulse, but, in order to suggest the possibilty of applying my philosophical attitude to poetry, I shall add a few remarks on *Paradise Lost*.

The discrepancy, with Milton, between observation and ideas, is best shown in his similes, for instance the bees at the beginning of Book IV. Milton had been a good observer of nature, but nature, serving as an imperfect illustration of theology, remains disembodied in the poem. But the majestic whole, united with the sublime tone, confers a final unity on such a vast allegory that nothing seems out of place: a common belief, a common tradition, a true observation of human character, a study of envy, pride, liberty, humility, obedience. It is possible to attack Milton's prosody and his abstract style, but impossible to attack him as a whole, for his poetry is pervaded with a sense of greatness that bathes the smallest detail and adorns the bare rhetoric of his dialogues. The sublime tone is sustained throughout the fable of *Paradise Lost;* the unprepared reader gets tired but will never deny the greatness and the strange attraction of the poem. A great defect of *Paradise Lost* as a work of art lies in the purely explanatory and ornamental part played by nature. But who, considering the other huge problems solved in that ambitious work, would wish to solve that problem also? It could even be argued that, in a subject-matter of that scope, nature could play no better part.

When all has been said for or against *Paradise Lost,* we are left with the strength of a proud mind who was not satisfied until he had told his whole truth. What is nobler than this refusal of the poets to leave this world before imparting a meaning, and what is reality if it does not mean anything?

What we give is not our own, but the meaning is created by us, and the meaning is always a meeting of the facts we are aware of and the spirit that dwells in us.

11. CONCLUSION

"OUR knowledge, therefore, is real only so far as there is a conformity between our ideas and the reality of things". This statement by Locke[1] could be taken as an epigraph for this book, although we should interpret it in a way which Locke would not have subscribed to. That vague conformity, which has led to Hume's scepticism, as well as the ambiguous use of the word 'real' show us that the whole difficulty comes from considering things—and reality—in themselves. Both Locke and Hume do this. Is it possible to disentangle anything from the knowledge or experience we have of it?

But it is no use trying to eradicate an illusion which has become almost the fundamental tenet and at the same time the death of philosophy, for if things exist exclusively by themselves, then what is the meaning, the use and the purpose of philosophy or, indeed, of any exercise of the mind?

Besides, if the nature of things is absolutely distinct from the intellect or intuition, there is no possibility of knowledge and consequently no philosophy: reality becomes a heap of phenomena without meaning, and philosophy a gratuitous and pointless play with false concepts.

The great majority of people feel that reality is terrible, and avoid it. They take refuge in habits and dogmas, and stop thinking as soon as a difficulty presents itself. They refuse to be responsible for their own life and, for their own safety, persuade others to refuse.

[1] *An Essay concerning Human Understanding*, Oxford, Clarendon Press, 1934, p. 288. The preceding sentence is: "It is evident the mind knows not things immediately, but only by the intervention of the ideas it has of them."

The weight of generations of thinkers who, from cowardice and desire for safety, have been led into accepting dogmas and things in themselves is so great that both refusals have acquired the force of authority and are considered as natural. They are nothing but obscurantism, and can only do harm.

It is significant to observe that those who have fixed (that is, killed) their thought for ever by accepting a set of dogmas embodied in a monumental doctrine, dismiss all philosophers —except the 'good' ones—as vague dreamers, and all poets without exception. They know it is better to kill what is best in themselves than to open their eyes. They would do any- thing for the sake of their creed, for truth is their enemy. They killed their thought, and therefore, from jealousy and fear, they want to kill other people's thought, pressing others to imitate their example and subjecting others to the authority of their beliefs.

The acceptance of dogmas and things in themselves hinders not only philosophy, but literature also. If things are things, and if truth is revealed and settled, why are we reading and writing, why are we living at all?

We cannot be indifferent to what men think and write, in the present and in the past. Fortunately, literary values are constantly revised and cannot become too much distorted. There is, however, one element in criticism that cannot be changed : works of literature are not judged by their con- formity with real things or, as Locke would have it, by "the agreement or disagreement of our own ideas"[2] : they are judged by the life of the spirit that is in them. Whether or not they agree with dogmas or with real things is irrelevant to their value. Neither the doctrinaires, whose thought is fixed, nor the materialists, who give up thinking, can in any way change this fact. They try to evade it, to criticize or to praise an author according to his conformity to dogmas or realities, but in vain. Literature escapes and transcends partial investi-

[2] op. cit. p. 287.

gations because it is an expression of the complete man. It is as impossible to deprive literature of its integrity as to dissect a living creature.

All works of literature are also imperfect, which means, first, that the notion of literature is associated with the notion of perfection, and secondly that the value of particular works depends on their relation to a general ideal perfection that is never realized. It would be presumptuous to say here—and impossible to define—what this perfection is. The infinite cannot be defined. But it must include a certain measure of insight, a certain penetration of the spirit, a certain presence of the spirit and of the world allied to a certain skill, so that perfection would be the full measure of these qualities.

For many reasons, no writer can reach perfection; first because no language is universal and permanent, and also because, whatever the scope of his culture, of the traditions he has assimilated, he is an individual; but what he has to say, what he communicates, is interesting in so far as it is an expression of the whole man, of universal perfection, for there is only one perfection.

We do not know this perfection (it is easier to know limitations) but we know well enough two things: first, that this perfection has been created little by little throughout the centuries by the writers themselves, and is made up, so to say, of the joint, incomplete perfection of all greater or lesser works; secondly, that this perfection, admitting whatever is living and true, tolerates neither limitations, intolerance, fixed thought, nor things in themselves.

A general philosophy of literature cannot be based upon any preconception; the only requisite is to realize—and to admit—that neither the spirit nor things exist in themselves, that no real thing can be separated from the notion, the perception, the fear or the hope of it, that literature is a human enterprise which humanizes the strangest and most indifferent things, finally that reality is meaning or—which is the same—that literature embodies reality, reality as matter, reality as death, reality as God, and reality as the living author.

We fear reality, we fear death, and we fear God. The simple prerequisite of our philosophy of literature is strangely unknown, but not so unknown that it may never bear fruit.

PART TWO

The Making of Literature

PHILOSOPHICAL CATEGORIES OF
LITERATURE

THE sole valuable criterion for literature, and indeed for all human productive work, is the spirit, but not the absolute spirit, the spirit in itself : the concrete, adapted, appropriate spirit.

As we have seen in the chapter on the ambivalence of literature, pure description is as vain—and as impossible—as discarnate, bodiless, immaterial spirituality. Literary creation is made of words, the symbols of things and feelings. An accumulation of facts or a mere statement of ideas is much less a creation that a technical construction with a purpose. Nature itself is devoid of the spirit—of meaning—only in so far as we do not understand, grasp or create it.

The value of a work of art is therefore measured by the presence of the creative spirit in it, that is, by a happy union between reality and awareness.

The words 'nature', 'spirit' and 'reality' are—fortunately— for ever vague, precisely because their meaning has to be created, and depends on an historical evolution of taste and culture. They are, however, the tools of criticism, and our philosophy of literature cannot do without them. They help us to distinguish those works that emphasize 'reality', or 'nature' from those that emphasize 'meaning' or 'the spirit'.

Above all, they enable us to criticize the works that fail to unite both elements and those that lack either of them. All these distinctions, however, are but steps in our search for the spirit as temporarily captured by one author and shared by us all, for the spirit is nothing but the timeless, purposeful and destiny-making man. We may invent a God in order to account for the spirit, but if we want to take our full share of responsibility, we must take upon ourselves the responsibility for guiding our world, which up to now has been an attribute of the gods. The individual man, who has accepted part of the total burden of creation, goes back to nature—disappears completely from the scheme of things—and is replaced by others like him who in their turn contribute to the complete man.

The whole man is therefore immanent, lives in this world, but at the same time he lives through all individual changes (birth, childhood, old age and death) and through history (buildings, peoples, languages, etc.).

The ultimate value of any work of literature lies in a presence of the whole man, in a merging of the time-bound reality into the whole man.

As I demonstrated in the chapter entitled Life and Literature, at the level of individual existence there are limited and hermetically closed and separate entities, whereas at the level of literature there is meaning, that is, correspondence, unity, harmony. There is no literature where there is no harmony, no unity where man is cut in two parts: the immanent self and the transcendental anti-self or, on a lower level, the sentimental self and the materialistic environment.

However harmonious his personality may be, man is in conflict with himself, but under various appearances and circumstances, it is always the tragic struggle between the time-bound man and the timeless man: that is the supreme subject-matter for all authors, whether poets, dramatists, novelists or critics.

The tragic end of the time-bound man is glorious when he

is sacrificed by himself. He always perishes; and according as he is put to death by himself, by others or by circumstances, we have tragedy, comedy or drama. The relation between the existing, moral individual and the immortal, impersonal spirit is the substance of all books, the literary reality. Social and cosmological relations are but secondary themes, and their problems are often badly stated, for the relations between an individual and another individual or group, both mortal and meaningless in themselves, are without significance, unless they lead to the discovery of the spiritual man, as they do in Molière's comedies.

Now, a great variety of attitudes is open to the whole, spiritual, real man : he may smile at his poor existing limited self, as Washington Irving does in his tales, or he may pity him, or be angry with him, but he cannot wholly identify himself with him. Even the romantic self, *'le moi'*, does not exactly represent the individual.

I have so far drawn two main distinctions : first, between the whole, active spirit and the immaterial, abstract mind (doctrines and systems); secondly between the whole man and the individual. A comparison of the two antitheses shows that man (the whole man) and the spirit have an essential duality in common. The whole man, being the motive and quintessence of history, is made of successive efforts, failures and achievements, whereas the spirit, being the awareness of something, creates, destroys and modifies its own object. History or nature cannot be conceived without man or the spirit.

It follows from this duality that literature, being meaning and transposition, offers an excellent meeting ground for the dual aspects of both man and the spirit, whose essence is meaning and relation.

The whole man has his moods, ranging, not from love to hatred, but from pity to impatience, according to his attitude toward the limited self. The spirit has various grades of elevation and purity, ranging from realism to meditation, according as the spirit or its object is predominant. Literature can be studied from these twin points of view : moods and grades.

In spite of the simplicity of these two criteria, they do not enable us to label any great work with a fixed category. Art escapes easy definitions. We can easily discern a dominant mood or a depth or range of awareness in a writer, but we cannot bind mood and grade together without recreating the work as it is, for unity is the characteristic law of art, and unity cannot be analysed without being destroyed. Art is unity, but a dual unity, duality of man and duality of the spirit. The whole man and the limited self, the conception and the things conceived : between the two terms of each anti-thesis, in equilibrium, lies the field of literature, between two sets of extremes to be reconciled.

It is therefore dangerous to overpraise either art or nature. The French classical doctrine of the seventeenth century was tacitly and expressedly based upon the motto : "imitate nature" ! That was perhaps the inevitable reaction from the artificial stiffness of the alexandrine and of the three unities. Art draws its substance from nature, whereas nature is an arti-ficial creation.

We are repeatedly assured by materialists or by religious thinkers that we live in obscurity, imprisoned by our body and our senses in a material world which we can neither know nor change. This is only half the truth, for we can no more escape from our *own* spirit than from nature : Neither of them offers any refuge : nature has to be created and conquered by the spirit, and we want to possess nature.

If this is our destiny, those Europeans who have become Americans may be said to have received a peculiar mission. In their search for liberty and in their desire to escape from the old world, they have conquered the new world. Two powerful and contradictory trends are felt in their life and in their literature; they want to escape into nature (Emerson, Thoreau, Melville, Hemingway, etc.), running away from their own civilization, and they want to give a spiritual value to their material civilization (Franklin, Whitman, William Saroyan, etc.). They are torn in two pieces, they are longing for home. Their home is both in the culture they have escaped from and in the land they are for ever discovering, conquering and settling. I am not suggesting that they are culturally Europeans. Their culture lies precisely in an equipoise between the ancient but still living tradition, and the new conditions of life. Their products seem strange and new to the European, who fails to recognize his own spirit. If the European does not want to drop behind, he has to follow or to take the lead, but in any event he suffers from the impression that he has given birth to his own master.

F

13. LIMITATIONS AND GREATNESS IN LITERATURE

(a) The Borders of Literature

TOPICAL writings and pure speculation are not literature, not at least when the first are without meaning and when the second is not sincere or translated into concrete images. The field of literature does not lie between these opposites, it lies where they meet.

It is commonly assumed that literature is neither purely topical nor purely speculative. A treatise on cooking does not belong to literature, unless the writer, say Brillat-Savarin, has endowed it with certain 'literary' qualities. The information given by newspapers and reviews, thousands of instructive or entertaining books, even scientific treatises fall short of what is required in literature. The same is true of many books on religion, theology, philosophy, politics and history. Calvin is a theologian in his *Institution chrétienne* and an artist in his *Petits Traités*. Both Dante and Milton are poets, but the theological elements in the *Divine Comedy* and in *Paradise Lost* are outside literature. Brillat-Savarin, on the one hand, and Calvin on the other hand, may be chosen as cases that mark the limits of literature.

Literature plays an extremely limited part in contemporary society. Information is what the people want, science what they need, and ideology what moves them. Though it may be tolerated as a relaxation or adornment—which it is not—literature is irrelevant to the concern of modern life. Information belongs to the press, science to the university, politics to the parties, religion to the churches, your body to the doctor and your soul to the psychoanalyst. If the spirit wants to play a part in this world, it must apply for a laboratory and produce a new technical device.

And yet, this society of specialists needs the writer who makes a synthesis, who gives a meaning to facts and who makes ideas human. It needs the presence of a man. All information on all subjects will add to knowledge but will not produce a wise man, and the triumph of ideology will not make anybody better or happier.

Literature has a place in this world, but not in the world of specialists. Literature binds and unites, reconciles opposites and transcends conflicts. The world falls apart. Ideologies poison millions of victims and the rest drown their indifference in a hand-to-mouth existence. Indifference, fanaticism and sentimentality go together. They are the negation of sensibility.

(b) Derivative Art

In the nineteenth century art became fictitious and superficial. The opera is typical of an empty period that demanded vast fabulations. The music of *La Traviata* is excellent, although at times sentimental, and the public weeps with *La Traviata,* but the whole is much ado about nothing.[1]

What does the public come for? I suppose that the public wants to bathe in a stream of music and to be overwhelmed by a show of costumes. It is an agreeable and innocent stream, interspersed with touches of creative genius, but unreal, unnecessary . . . The tears and the ecstasy were not true; only the senses, the merely *receptive* senses were alive, or rather functioning, flowing with the stream.

The same criticism applies still more to the cinema and to

[1] See Hermann Broch, Dichten und Erkennen, Rhein-Verlag, Zürich, 1955, pp. 71. 72 and 73.

television. The public has become passive and receptive. We are tired. People want images and sounds. The artist cannot create when the people want him to produce. The artist has become difficult, and the public is tired. You cannot create for a public that does not exist or understand.

This need for sounds and images is a substitute for the word. All the shows, all the speed and the excitement hide a deep inner emptiness. The senses keep functioning, and with them the machines, the factories, the planes and the ships. The landscape rolls past you as you drive, and you feel strong, but you are driven forward and the power is no longer under your control. You are passive and excited, objective and empty.

We lose control, while the machines, the sounds and the images drive us in many directions. We create energy, and the energy turns against us. We have to create, take over and control the world, for there is no other world than our world, one great man's world.

Art is the symbol, not the mirror of society, of its shortcomings and its virtues. There is only one literature and one taste; literatures and tastes pass away. The grasp of reality is always partial, so long at least as society remains unbalanced and art incomplete, but the control of the world is man's task and need. There is no escape, and the only means of achieving control is greatness in the use of the word, or the building of a comprehensive substance from symbols. The intermediate reality of symbols is the only bridge between the empty world and the dispossessed spirit, and the only means of capturing reality.

(c) Money

Money is a source of power and control, for money is the exchange-rate or intermediate stage in a huge metamorphosis ranging from the work of the farm hand to the gold held in the banks. Everybody is involved in the economic circuit, both as consumer and producer, but money alone does not reflect the whole process, and therefore does not capture reality. Even in economics, money is not all, and you cannot foresee the future in terms of money. A farmer's horse or tractor may be translated into terms of money, but then that is far from being the whole story.

There is only one means of exchange for reality : the word. Things and beings meet the sentient man in the word. The word shapes the aspect of the world and supplies the presence of the spirit.

Money accounts for the so-called material values, that is, for property, raw materials, labour, other services, etc. I suppose that an economist would be more competent here, and that we are on fairly conjectural and controversial ground. What interests us, however, and what can hardly be disputed, is that money is—or should be—common. The trouble with money is that there is always too little or too much of it. The just distribution of money, representing material goods, is what people need and often desire.

Now literature does not bestow the same powers and rights as money, does not represent the same things, and is not the same means of exchange. It would be too simple a commonplace to say that money represents material goods, and literature spiritual goods. For example, the usefulness of a few purely intellectual and less purely spiritual services is recognized sufficiently, for them to bring in money[1]. However it may be, it is dangerous and ridiculous to see nothing in literature but pure spirit. There is no pure literature and a pure spirit does not exist[2]. Literature, like money, is a means of exchange, but money stands for common, usually material or temporal goods (or evils), whereas literature offers some values representing, not the common, but the rare goods, not the measurable, but the imponderable goods.

[1] "As far as we know, Shakespeare always worked for money, giving the best of his intellect to support his trade as an actor." Trollope, *An Autobiography*, London, Williams & Norgate, 1946, p. 106.
[2] "Plato himself is said to have lived with a good deal of magnificence." Adam Smith, *The Wealth of Nations*, Everyman's Library, vol. 1, p. 122.

(d) Literature not common

That literature is no common and no measurable means of exchange has never been—and cannot be—generally understood. In an era like ours, in which the sense of values is weakened and men are treated as masses or economic factors, the familiarity and power of what is common or coarse are so strong that we cannot retain a sense of the value of what is rare, precious, and supreme. Literature is one of those precious things that are never valued by common people; they value money and treasure it.

The modern writer, on the contrary, who, if he appeals to the common man, must sacrifice the value of what he writes, is acutely aware of the uncommon character of his work, and sometimes deliberately writes for a select public and shocks those outside. Hermetism, the æsthetics for the happy few, salvation for the elected adepts, literature for those who have the same political training and convictions, none of these exclusive types of literature is likely to reach the proper audience, to divest the common man of his coarseness, to give him a sense of what is precious, and to present him with the rare gift.

It is of no use to argue about the utility of literature, to dismiss it on the ground that it is not meant for the common man and the common good, to proclaim the birth of a popular literature and to order poets to sing of the charms and achievements of the nation. The "great"[3] writers have never praised the common, except when they have seen something precious in it.[4]

---

[3] This adjective, implying a measure, is wrongly applied to the measureless *par excellence*.

[4] Here we may think of Wordsworth, but also of the Victorian novelists, especially George Sand. See in this respect La Crisi dell' Eroe nel Romanzo Vittoriano, by Mario Praz. Translated by Angus Davidson, O.U.P., London: Cumberlege, 1956.

If, however, a proof is needed, I shall supply an example of the unfortunately not rare fallacy of setting a high value on common qualities. I am very anxious to show that what is ordinary or common does not belong to literature, and, like money, has a low and transitory value.

Here is my illustration. In his useful book entitled *Aspects of the Modern Short Story*,[5] Alfred C. Ward hails Stacy Aumonier as a major writer who "should take a high place in a period which marks the renascence of the short story." In contradiction to the "high place" and to the final remark that "his pen has qualities which command attention and admiration on account of some specially meritable feature", we learn that "he (Stacy Aumonier) has made himself acceptable to the magazine public without writing down to any presumed 'magazine standard'. His gifts are catholic and he is among the very best equipped short-story writers of the younger generation. If he has not the special powers which belong to a few of his contemporaries, he has conversely the advantage of not being a writer for an exclusive coterie." Now what matters, the magazine with the large number of common readers, or "the special powers"? You cannot have it both ways. The common taste is no taste at all.

I am sorry to deal at length with a rather weak chapter on a minor author (and I have nothing *against* minor authors), but I am justified because the common and the ordinary serve to determine what literature is not. Alfred C. Ward is well aware of the importance of "the special powers", but he effortlessly and vulgarly errs in praising his author for introducing commonplace, ordinary and familiar subject-matter. We learn that "Stacy Aumonier might be termed the Prose Laureate of the Inarticulate Ones", but who today, thirty years after so much popularity and well earned money, after so many tears, who reads or hears of Stacy Aumonier and his common, inarticulate people?

Two salient features of Alfred C. Ward's critical attitude

[5] University of London Press, 1924.

are worth mentioning here. First, he calls Shakespeare to witness in the introduction and the conclusion of his chapter.
Shakespeare may serve many causes, and false ones among
them : "The strange and the rare and the precious have a
place in literature, but it should not be forgotten that Shakespeare . . ."

Secondly, the strange and the rare and the precious, for
Alfred C. Ward, are not the qualities that distinguish a rare
author; these words refer exclusively to the subject-matter.
Alfred C. Ward is entirely concerned with subject-matter,
although he mentions what he characteristically terms "style
and so on".[6] He claims that "style and so on" were important in the past, but what matters today is sentiment, not to be
"tragically" mistaken for sentimentality.

Here again we are faced with the dichotomy mentioned in
my chaper on Life and Literature. Style is a strange animal.
The common man wants tears and style and so on, otherwise
literature is no use to him. And Alfred C. Ward, who needs
something more, looks for sentiment and reality, common
reality, not true reality. For him, what is interesting in a short
story is not the short story, but its subject-matter, here for instance : "the almost unbearable stirring of emotion produced
by the author through this character is due not at all to her
words, but wholly to the fact that grief has made her incap-
able of speech". Alfred C. Ward speaks of the characters as
of real persons, not as of characters. A cat is a cat and a character is a character, but our critic, like many critics and most
common readers, does not accept this commonplace. It is too
hard a truth for his tears, his sentiment and his burning,
crowded imagination.

A second instance of this morbid interest in subject-matter :
"Lastly, of *Them Others* it must be emphasized (for the en-
couragement of readers who shrink from 'painful' subject-
matter in fiction) that Mrs. Ward is not a depressing character. If she were, the story would be negligible". But the most

[6] p. 242 of his book.

uproariously comic instance, the third and last one, is that of a character who "is a joy to those Londoners who are familiar with fried-fish shop procedure". Here we have the select reader, here the strange and the rare and the precious have a place in literature!

14. THE ELUSIVE SYNTHESIS

THE purpose of this book is not to find out what the spirit or matter is. No definition will hold true. I am satisfied with pointing out that the relations between the spirit and matter are reality, a reality that eludes all investigations concerned exclusively with its appearance or its substance, a reality created and achieved, not reproduced or imitated, in the meaning of a work of art.

The reader may object here that a work of art is necessarily limited in scope and catches only one part or aspect of reality. This is too naïve and quantitive. The scope of any work is limited, but what should not be limited is the meaning. The smallest event can acquire a universal meaning, and, once more, the event is no reality in itself, unless it implies both what happens and the awareness of what happens.

Various degrees and forms of awareness are distinguished, and there are events of different ranges of importance. The dangerous thing is to consider by itself either the awareness or the events.

History as a whole is not so much a slow scientific progress (as the U.N.E.S.C.O. would have it), as a struggle of the spirit—the human variety of the universal spirit—for mastery, control and harmony. This trend of the spirit—its very essence —is sometimes turned aside into a struggle for annihilation and loneliness.

To create an artificial civilization is not the greatest thing we can do, it is to grasp reality; the unpredictable, unrealized reality that escapes the longest treatises and the most realistic novels.

Meaning is life, deep life, and thought, consistent thought. It is life and thought blended into the same substance: the unsaid, unutterable reality, or the word, the meaning of a life's work and the book that is life.

It is evident that our philosophy of literature comes from two sources—beside my own view of the subject—the authors' explicit statements and their works: their thought, and the life their works are endowed with. There can hardly be much discrepancy between the philosophical utterances, if any, of a great writer and their æsthetic illustration.[1] An author's views on life and art are useful to us, though at times they have an indirect relation to his work. They are at least interesting to the philosopher in so far as they correspond to the contents of the work or are part of it and help us to understand it.

Sometimes, as with the Victorian sages[2], they defy any abstract formulation. Nevertheless, they are views on life and are formulated in the writer's work itself. We must therefore concentrate on the work without forgetting that it is essentially a *message*. If we wish to show that such messages are of doubtful validity, this should be done, not by reducing them to preposterous ideas, but by showing that the characters and incidents in the novels, or the historical pictures (in Carlyle) are ridiculous and unlikely.

[1] Wyndham Lewis seems to be an exception to this rule. The anonymous reviewer of the T.L.S. of August 2, 1957, stresses the romanticism of this would-be classic.

[2] cf. *The Victorian Sage,* by John Holloway, London, Macmillan, 1953.

15. LITERATURE AND SCIENCE

WE cannot determine the extent of our knowledge until we see it expressed. Dictionaries contain dead knowledge only. The most real knowledge is that contained in words, made into a symbol, in which the real and the speculative are one.

The knowledge so defined is rare. Only in moments of great awareness can the writer attain it. It has characteristic intensity, vividness and comprehensiveness. It may be expressed in abstract words or notions, and yet it is neither abstract, nor lifeless.

I do not question the validity of science, but I do not believe that biology will ever account for life as long as science remains objective and accumulative. You cannot pin down life, or stop reality; you cannot put aside the basic fact of time, and time eludes the objective attitude, the scientific method of analysing, measuring, accumulating and counting.

When everything else has left your consciousness, you are left with an awareness of time. Time is an awareness of mere passing. Not passing : the feeling or dreaming or realizing of passing. So time depends on you, that is, on your being subject to it, on your suffering from or profiting by it. Time is always yours, an infinite possibility; there is always something possible, something new, and you are always making something out of it. The repetition and the uniformity of life are artificial children of boredom; behind their lifeless façade you will find the abyss of perpetual invention, helplessness or resourcefulness, possibilities, indeterminacy, metamorphosis, in short : open time.

Time is open and unaccounted for. In order to grasp time,

you have to be time. What are uniformity and boredom, if not failure to live, failure to be up to the possibilities of time? For time is *infinite* and requires invention, not repetition but continuous creation. Time requires your contribution, your at least existing, your interrupted consciousness, time wants your whole life, which is not merely your daily work, your habits or what has become familiar to you; for your whole life is your spirit, what you have perhaps never achieved in spite of the infinite possibilities open to you.

In literature, we have no doubt an achievement of the spirit pregnant with time. There is no net that can catch time, for time must be lived, it involves the subject and is no object. Literature contains simultaneously the life of the subject and the reality of time. The ambivalence of literature is what makes it real. Time must be lived, and either you are forced to live it and you merely exist, work and suffer, or you give it your life, your spirit, and you create it.

This is no moral distinction : it is simply more comfortable to be lived than to create life. All creators are a menace to the established institutions. What society approves of, it calls good. Nevertheless, I am not speaking of an absolute : I suggest that the supreme degree of life is creation, and that therefore a high value must be set on literature. To determine the modes and grades of creation in each work calls for much patience and careful, detailed study. Will anyone deny that literature necessarily involves a kind of creation, an active contribution to life which, in its turn, involves a creation of time outside passive time?

Because of its creative element, literature is more likely than inventive science to approach reality, for the living reality could be grasped only by a purely and wholly creative act of the spirit. The complete reality is the spirit, all the possibilities and ways of the spirit animating nature. It might be added that existing things and beings disappear as such in the complete reality, but this would not alter the fact that we experience existence as separated, and that the complete reality is for us merely a conjecture. I have already shown that it is a necessary conjecture, and I have just argued that, whatever else we do, we must create. Imitation of others, habits, rites and conventions are a veil protecting us from creative effort and from the light of truth.

Something of the blinding light of reality is stored in books. Not the full light, but even the smallest spark is precious, though it may be obscured by the sweeping wind of the centuries. Each man carries the weight of the whole world on his spiritual wings. Most men, of course, prefer to stick to the ground. Some try to soar and fail and despair, others flutter around like chickens, and boast; they are all too heavy. Finally there are the rare ones who ascend with the whole weight of reality because they are light.

These old, worn-out and misused allegories of light and of wings may still point out one rule in the game of literature : the lighter you are, the more you gather. Writers who disregard this rule will soon disappear from the book shelves; they are those who gather too much material, and those who neglect, overlook or distort their materials.

The main philosophical difference between science and literature is that science consists in the observation of given materials, and that literature involves the full responsibility of the writer towards his subject-matter. No one will question Galileo's right to derive a revolutionary conclusion from the observation of facts, for the scientist is right when his observations are confirmed by facts. Not so with the writer, who is the author of his materials, for he chooses, invents, arranges and interprets them.

We have, or at least we think we have a clear notion of what a scientific discovery means. Literary invention is not so simple a concept. Whether the subject-matter is grand or new or fashionable is no criterion of value. The subject-matter is not given, it has to be made. With the same plot you can make a vulgar or an excellent play; from the same state of mind you can start an empty, unpoetic poem or a masterpiece. The word 'masterpiece' suggests mastery of both the feelings and the materials through which feelings are expressed. But it is wrong to speak of two identical states of mind, for no work of value is based upon a common state of mind.

For the scientist, there is only one logical conclusion, but several different works may result from the same influence. What is logical, common and communicable in literature is the least characteristic of its elements. The root of literature is its uniqueness, the rare quality without which the same things could be said by somebody else. This applies also to those scientific discoveries that are the fruit of genius as well as patient work, and only the scientific act of genius can be compared with literary creation, for the same discovery is subsequently used, applied, formulated and interpreted by others, until it is made available to thousands of students.

16. GENIUS

WE learn much from literature, but we do not learn how to write a masterpiece, unless 'we' become unique. There are common elements but the person of the writer is unique. I do not suggest that his life or his faculties must be exceptional, but that he must have an exceptional grip of his subject. His is a responsibility shared by very few. When we speak of an author's world, we understand that he is responsible for its creation. Whether that world exists or not is beside the question.

We live in unreality and vagueness. We dimly perceive half the truth. It is characteristically vague to believe that reality must be plain and common and simple. Reality is hidden and exceptional and difficult. When I say that the secret—or the uniqueness—of a masterpiece resides in the person of the writer, I do not suggest that the writer must be an exceptional person with an exceptional experience. What is exceptional is the understanding displayed by that person in his work. As a man, the writer may be a common, uninteresting and disagreeable person. His biography will not explain the secret of his success as a writer. We—the common people—are not real and live without reality, whereas those to whom a sense of reality is least attributed, the poets, are precisely those whose person becomes reality, those who most successfully reach the highest slopes of that difficult peak, reality.

The best proof that reality is almost unattainable is that it is unpredictable, and the most unpredictable of all realities, the least known of all, is man. As they are ignorant of themselves, 'common' people are open to all sorts of beliefs, un-controllable impulses, moral and political passions. They cannot reach the real and know themselves because they do not know the essential fact about themselves: that they are the authors of their life.

Since they shirk this fundamental responsibility, they are easy prey for more or less legitimate authorities and leave the conduct of events to the Almighty, to fate or to a powerful party doctrine. The more inhuman the authority or the doctrine, the more they believe in it. The result of such blindness is that, instead of being guided by the dark external powers they believe in, they are vanquished by their inner selves, the thing they least rely on. Possibly there is a conspiracy between the forces of nature and those of the spirit.

The exceptional, the rare and the unique is what we call personal genius. But there are many fallacies about genius, and one of the most dangerous is hero-worship. All these fallacies have in common a tendency to turn genius into an object, into something superhuman or at least extra-human. An object or a god, the divine subtracted from man (God is a subtraction, an abstraction and a theft). What is this personal genius but the most intimate self related to or identified with the wide world, a form of what Kierkegaard would call love? *The strangest things have a curious affinity with the most intimate ones.* I say intimate, not familiar or common, for familiar or common things can *be* strange.

To sum up, a masterpiece is the fruit of genius, that is, of a rare sense of an unpredictable reality which, if analysed, is found to consist in a conjunction of the inner self with the strange world. The force driving the individual genius to this conjunction is love, neither physical love between persons nor abstract, theological love, but the love enacted on the meeting ground of the inner and the outer worlds, within the framework of the conventional symbols at our disposal: words.[1]

G

The conclusion to be drawn from all this is perhaps that genius is the most common thing we can have, not common in the sense of usual or actually shared by all (for, as we have seen, it is quite the contrary) but common in the sense of virtually and absolutely shared by all, and akin to both man and the world : genius is the most congenial, cognate and related thing we can imagine. It is essentially related-ness, love *par excellence,* the two kin worlds made one. In this love meet not the surfaces, but the most intimate, hidden, dissimilar, remote, unexpected and unknown searchings in a certain arrangement of words that has both the fixity of a shot animal and the panting breath of a passionate quest : permanent and lively words.

[1] "To make the external internal, the internal external, to make nature thought and thought Nature—this is the mystery of genius in the fine arts." Coleridge, *Biographia.*

In a sense, literary creation is a typically, indeed supremely scientific, activity, for, if the reader agrees with me that the writer of genius does not create something absolutely new, but calls to his mind the unattainable reality (the real being his intimate experience), then literary creation is not only a kind of statement of what really is, but also no creation at all. We call it creation because we have to invent reality, because what is nearest and most evident to us is what most escapes our understanding. Familiar scenes, when a meaning is given to them, will seem the strange fruit of an exceptionally creative effort. Examples of this abound; but it is perhaps enough to mention one of those familiar landscapes through which Shakespeare provides a natural scenery adapted to the action of the play:

King Henry—
>How bloodily the sun begins to peer
>Above yon basky hill! the day looks pale
>At this distemperature.

Prince Henry—
>The southern wind
>Doth play the trumpet to his purposes;
>And by his hollow whistling in the leaves
>Foretells a tempest and a blustering day.

King Henry—
>Then with the losers let it sympathize,
>For nothing can seem foul to those that win.[1]

[1] First part of *King Henry IV*, Act V, Scene I.

Compare this dramatic scenery with a passage from Thackeray:

' "O those stars, those stars," Miss Rebecca would say, turning her twinkling green eyes up towards them. "I feel myself almost a spirit when I gaze upon them."

' "O—ah—God—yes, so do I exactly, Miss Sharp," the other enthusiast replied. "You don't mind my cigar, do you, Miss Sharp?" Miss Sharp loved the smell of a cigar out of doors beyond everything in the world—and she just tasted one too, in the prettiest way possible, and gave a little puff, and a little scream, and a little giggle, and restored the delicacy to the Captain, who twirled his moustache, and straightway puffed it into a blaze that glowed quite red in the dark plantation, and swore—"Jove —aw—God—aw—it's the finest segaw I ever smoked in the world aw," for his intellect and conversation were alike brilliant and becoming to a heavy young dragoon." [2]

These two quotations seem to have nothing in common, except that they establish a relation between the landscape and the characters. In spite of their dissimilarity, they have something essential in common, and I might have chosen other passages from very different authors to show the same striking quality: the intense, strange intimacy that these authors give to life. An analysis of Shakespeare's poetry, of Thackeray's irony, and of the artistic mastery of both, in handling only particulars, would stop short of disclosing the hidden source of genius.

The essential thing about Shakespeare and Thackeray is that they are responsible for their creation, a statement that can be analysed in two parts: first they re-create a world, and secondly they live in it, they are present. Detailed analysis will show the distinct presence of the characters and of nature, but the immediate and final readings will reveal one single

[2] *Vanity Fair*, Vol. I, end of chapter XI.

presence: that of the author. In so much infinitely patient work the author is absent that we should appreciate the responsibility where we find it! Even when they deal with familiar scenes, some authors go deep enough to find and bring back their truth; we rely upon them because of their responsibility, because they lead us somewhere else and where we are, because of the meaning they have found, the distant, intimate reality.

The "hollow whistling" or "a little puff" affect us, because they are not gratuitous. They have a value, a meaning, a place in the drama and in the novel. Frightful events may rage without leaving a trace in human memory. How many unrecorded changes the world has undergone! The interest of the "whistling" and of the "puff" lies in the attention paid to them. There lies also their reality. Nothing is humble or grand in itself, *we* make things so. Nothing lives, nothing is real unless we take upon ourselves the life and the reality. But where are life and reality, if they are neither in the world nor in ourselves, if neither the world nor we are real alone? I shall answer not that they are in the personality of the author, but that the author invests himself with them in his work.

The fundamental characteristic of any valuable work is that it is a monument of reality. The genius is the exceptional person who has been able to build it up, but the very fact that he is exceptional is rather a limitation: the full measure of reality could be attained only in a view of the whole world accepted by all men. But that is a hypothetical consideration: in fact and fortunately, the more exceptional the author, the more he approaches universality.

Ages, worlds and peoples can exist and have existed without the help of any writer, but they are lost, and have no significance or reality; reality begins when we become responsible for our own life, and it is perfected in creation. In spite of the variety of their works, Shakespeare and Thackeray construct comparatively little reality, and if their vision, already exceptional, had been still wider, they would be more universal, and we should recognize better in their works the possibilities of our existence.

In any reality there is an element of consciousness, not simply a consciousness that envelopes brute reality (the only envelope is the language), but the matrix and the life-giving force; not the acute observation or the exact statement, but the spirit from which matter receives its very substance and without which whatever exists (in the sense of what is given, things and beings in their brute condition) is unregenerated, un-re-created, unreal.

Not only men, but animals, plants and stones are endowed with spirit. Each humble plant has to re-create its possibilities. But man is different in that he is not confined to his narrow environment and is free to exercise his powers far from his confining body, free to create a world, and to become its master. Such is his spiritual power. As to material power, again it is nothing if not created and mastered; in itself it is like an instrument without a master.

This does not mean that man is to become the absolute master of the earth, perhaps even of other worlds, or of the universe. It means that, within the universe (whether the universe exists or not does not matter), man may create a valid world, that is, valid for him, where he may live, a reality. His struggle is against unreality, absence and unrecorded time. Defeat for him is to fail to make the world, his life and even his death his own. Man has always tried to transform his death into a triumph, inventing myths of resurrection; but the most pregnant of all myths is that of Prometheus, for it involves the whole of human destiny and points out the fundamental meaning of life.

What indeed is our purpose, our primordial need, our *sine qua non* condition if not to steal fire? The fire of life, the fire of the spirit that means life and creates the unpredictable reality, the fire that we still leave to those creatures of ours, the gods? For if we do not take on ourselves their powers, we are obliged to invent substitutes to act for us, and substitutes are sometimes treacherous. Let us hope that men will have the courage to be responsible for the whole of reality and will no longer attribute it to the gods that they have invented to explain away their failures. This change is perhaps a law of evolution. Primitive peoples are the most religious; the history of nations begins in religious infancy. Art and literature, too, have religious origins. Religion is necessary to compensate for man's lack of understanding; it is necessary because it is man's destiny to accept the whole burden or to be crushed by it. I do not say that man has more and more understanding, but that he is increasingly obliged to face his responsibilities alone. A violent rejection of religion leaves a dangerous emptiness.

Our spiritual possibilities are infinite, and we hardly make use of them; as to our physical and material possibilities, they generally are used to the full, and the resulting exhaustion weakens our mastery over the world.

But we have strayed far from literature, and it is no use saying things : it is much more important to make them. This philosophy of literature should not consist in a series of general statements and detailed studies, leading to abstract theories : I have to make, not a book about literature, but literature itself. Thousands of books are published every year, but where is literature? Certainly not in these thousands, for few of them, perhaps not one, are characterized by unity, permanence, universality, uniqueness and genius. Large publics prefer third-rate products, but in spite of their contempt for or indifference to literature, there is in the long run no value in what they like, pay for, understand and demand. The favour of the public is no criterion.

Whereas the critic marks out those few books that are endowed with a lasting value, the philosopher of literature contributes to the creation of literature. Although he cannot change a word of what has been written, he must create, just as the authors had to create their reality. It is not sufficient for him to interpret the finished work, he must first take account of the creative force; what is more, he must himself invent the reality of literature. It is often taken for granted that literature as such exists, but few realize that its existence is the product of a huge, continuous and collective process. If we should start to believe in our literature, revere it as sacred and interpret it as the voice of God, then we should have holy scriptures or ideologies that would hinder and determine all further developments. There is another attitude still more dangerous: to dismiss our literature as a thing of the past, to stop interpreting it. Fanaticism, because of its positive element, causes perhaps less damage than oblivion.

A masterpiece is a creation; so is also literature as such, for the simple reason that literature is made of all the masterpieces, added together and made into a whole. In effect a masterpiece shaped from various other masterpieces, literature is in search of an author. Much reading, good taste and, above all, the creative powers of a wide personality, are required if literature is to become a reality.

18. THE TRANSCENDENTAL PERSON
OF THE AUTHOR

Now we may ask who unites all these qualities. Is it a single person or a collective association? It is both of them and more: it is a transcendental personality. When commenting upon Shakespeare and Thackeray, I mentioned various characteristics of genius, that exceptional magnet that draws everything to the call of one person. One more characteristic is to be emphasized: the transcendental element. Thackeray as a man is different from Thackeray as an author. The reader is primarily interested in Thackeray as an author, and we may go so far as to say that the reader is not interested at all in Thackeray; he is interested in the story, the characters, the style, the scenes and the times portrayed by Thackeray. All this makes the trancendental personality of Thackeray; it is not Thackeray in himself, limited to what is strictly personal to him, but Thackeray's world bearing Thackeray's imprint. If a short definition is asked for, I would say that an artist's transcendental person is whatever appears in his presence. It is not so much himself as the objects he has created, the things that could not exist without him. This is in agreement with my epistemology (theory of knowledge and reality), with my claim that reality depends on the knowledge or perception of reality and is neither purely a thing (materialism) nor purely a thought (absolutism), but both. For those who study literary reality from this point of view, the importance of what I call the author's transcendental person is evident.

I shall not make the mistake of attributing an absolute

value to literature. It would be dangerous to believe that, because a genius is exceptional, only a genius is capable of creating a reality. I maintain that a genius creates *his* reality, an independent reality, and that the personality of common people is too weak, not conscious or creative enough to grasp and personify much reality. They are satisfied with their immediate or immanent personality, but not even common people can be simply what they are, they must make themselves, and where will they find the necessary creative impulse if not in the active process underlying literature, philosophy, science, art and religion?

It is all very well not to be responsible for reality, but if you do not act, you suffer; if you are concerned exclusively with your immediate needs, you lose touch with reality and become lifeless, rotten, passive, an economic factor. It is not surprising that the growth of the industrial proletariat should have inspired the Marxist doctrine, but we should not believe that man, in the long run, will be content to play the part of an economic factor. The condition, the will and the need of every man is to create, to make his life, his world, his work. The whole point lies in the interpretation of the possessive "his". If he thinks of himself as an individual, as a member of a political party or of a church, as a citizen or even as the promoter of a broad civilization, he will certainly be disappointed : his life will hardly turn out as he wishes. The word "his" refers to the transcendental person we have mentioned.

Every man partakes, actively and passively, consciously and unconsciously, of the transcendental person. Everyone creates a certain reality and assumes a certain responsibility. The most exceptional and individual genius draws his strength from some universal source rather than from his peculiarities. The apparent peculiarity of some authors like Oscar Wilde and William Butler Yeats can be ascribed to the fact that they acted their lives and wore a mask; their person is acquired; we cannot say that Yeats had a spontaneous genius like Shelley's. Genius can be spontaneous in one sense: coming from itself, from the creative self. With Shelley, the creative self is perhaps emphasized at the expense of the result of creation, although much in him has been acquired.

19. EXPRESSION

THE transcendental self is the person hidden, latent, virtual, behind all things, which alone makes things and events into realities. In literature, that self has its means of becoming public, evident and real, of expressing itself. The process of literary expression, when there is real expression, is simply the realization of the transcendental self. But the whole of what we usually call reality, of unknown things and unpredictable events, of society and nature, remains unrealized. Hence the tendency to attribute it to an unknown person named God. Unknown, but known to those who believe in revelation or to experts in mysticism or in pantheism.

The whole of what we usually call reality may then be compared with a masterpiece that has not found its author and may be conceived as the unexpressed realization of the collective, impersonal, transcendental self. That reality is indissolubly linked with a sense of human failure or, what amounts to the same thing, with a sense of the divine. Even the genius has that sense when he is conscious of his limitations, for the whole universe is a personal affair, not an individual one.

What I have just said may serve to suggest that the more personal and transcendental the creator (that is, a man, for every one, not only the artist, is and must be a creator), the less he is individual and engaged. By "engaged" I imply the tendency to accept established institutions, doctrines, views and ideologies and to contribute to them passively. The general passivity of men explains the dangerous but vain power of uniform theories, slogans and authorities. But passivity does not release men from their creative task. It is not enough to be engaged in life, one has to give life, to become the life-giving person; both by realizing life, by expression, and by suffering life, by trial and judgment, attributing responsibility not to others, to the powerful, to God, but to one's conscience and unused possibilities. Powers and deities inherit their being from the transcendental person, when it fails to create by itself.

It is impossible to say exactly what the transcendental person is. It is not, it creates. Nevertheless, if an example is wanted, literature will yield many, because it is the best means of expression. There the hidden person is realized, there worlds have acquired a personality. It is easier to say what the transcendental person is not: not an identification with certain trends of opinion, the voice of a party, of a system, of anything established, fixed and precluding creation, therefore precluding the human person.

20. HISTORY

THE success of most contemporary books is largely due to their flattering and established moral, social or political prejudice. Many prizes are awarded to those that deserve well of a literary school vaguely linked with some unnamed authority, but how many are awarded for the sake of literature? And yet time works a wonderful change, blotting out the influence of politics and time-bound criteria, sifting real from established values, emphasizing the creative element. Very few books can withstand this process. The dead leaves return to the soil and the ever-present plants are called forth by the timeless eye, the function of which is not to receive visual perceptions, but to cause things to appear, so that what is most real for contemporaries, what exists and forces itself upon them as long as they remain passive, disappears in the night of oblivion. But the things and beings caught by the creative eye live for ever.

To apply these remarks to history my lead us astray. Very many unrecorded events have occurred and the portions of time that have been written about are relatively minute; our historical notions apply almost exclusively to those selected times and our interest concentrates on the famous leaders of peoples. We should not think that only these famous people have existed, only these glorious events have happened, but one thing we observe : that not only the future and the present, but also the past is what we make it. Which of us is it that makes the past? The one who is least considered by his contemporaries, the historian. If we think that what will remain of our present time depends on him, we should be more prudent, erect a statue to our future historian, and take care that we attract his attention, if we want to exist, to be real, not simply to have existed and to be dead!

What, to us, are the millions of centuries behind and before us if they never reach the threshold of our consciousness? They *are* unreal. Explorers do not pierce the secret of places and phenomena that already exist; they make real what had been thought unreal. The more we use our powers to make things real, the more we are living and real. There are two kinds of powers: those we accept because we cannot help it, and those that we lay hold on. As far as the present is concerned, we are overwhelmed by a sense of our impotence, we listen passively to the news without knowing that we are responsible for the events we are told of. And yet, for everyone able to detach his eyes from the immediate present, the strange blind force of events is nothing compared to a breath of the spirit, to one creative sign, to the presence of a timeless person. What is ultimately real is not what we think is real, but what we make real. Even the most external and present event is of our making, and past, forgotten prehistories are waiting for us. We suffer and create, for the worlds cannot revolve of themselves. They can revolve without our flesh, not without our spirit.

21. RESURRECTION

THE inevitable, indispensable spirit is what proclaims the value of literature. Through it we live, we are made by it, and yet we are rarely moved by it. The general indifference to literature is as great as the immense value of the neglected works. What are centuries of primitive life compared to one creative act? In the narrow cave of Altamira a world is opened. Life is there, not in the busy towns.

All this reminds us that, of the thousands of printed books, few kindle the timeless flame of life. The invisible, tiny, precious flame burns under heaps of burnt-out words. Such is the limitation and the glory of literature: when everything else has expired, the minute fire is still ready to evoke the only, the whole reality.

The fact of a re-birth through literature has never been appropriately observed by philosophers, although it is both the justification of literature and a very notable phenomenon from the philosophical point of view. I suppose that most readers, looking for a protection against what they take as their everyday reality, would prefer literature to be unreal: indeed they indulge in the most fantastic kinds of literature, which have no justification except that they correspond to a need, a passion or a weakness in the readers. Cheap novels, magazine stories, rosy poetry and detective stories, to choose some examples of derivative literature, show the philosopher what literature is not.[1] Yet many writers are acutely aware of

---

[1] "Stulta est clementia, cum tot ubique vatibus occurras, periturae parcere chartae." Juvenal, Satire 1, 17, 18.

a re-birth in their works, not only those who write about the past, the historians, and the authors of memoirs, but also the novelists, the dramatists and the poets.

The frailty of life and the necessity of re-birth is a familiar theme, not so much among Christian poets, whose religion does not allow them to deal profanely with it, as among the Ancients. Thus Catullus on his brother's death:

> *Ergo ego te audiero nunquam tua facta loquentem?*
> *Nunquam ego te, vita frater amabilior,*
> *Aspiciam posthac? At certe semper amabo:*
> *Semper maesta tua carmina morte canam;*
> *Qualia sub densis ramorum concinit umbris*
> *Daulias, absumpti gemeus Ityos . . .*[2]

Lyrical poets, singing of their love, seek their inspiration, not in the beloved one, but in the Muses, for they know that nobody will listen to them merely because they claim that their beloved was an exceptional beauty. So Propertius, afraid lest Cynthia might die:

> *Sunt apud infernos tot milia formosarum:*
> *Pulchra sit in superis, si licet, una locis . . .*[3]

The same Propertius, using a classical device, lets Cornelia's shade speak. What is this poet doing, if not causing the dead to live again? Many illustrations of this literary function could be given, such as Lucian's *Dialogues of the Dead*, Fontenelle and Fénelon's *Dialogues des Morts*.

This function of making the past and the dead live again is officially attributed to sculpture, when the statue of a great man, or a monument to commemorate a notable event, is ordered by some authority, erected and unveiled with enthusiastic speeches. But it is not often that the monument

[2] L XV, 9-14.
[3] Elegies, II, XXVIII, 49-50.

H

draws its artistic value from specific events that it recalls. The memories attached to the great man, the battle or the event misinterpret the memorial, for these memories may belong to the dead past. A true work of art creates a new life.

Less material than sculpture, literature is better equipped for this task. The word is subtler than concrete forms and gestures, however deep their meaning may be. Abstractions and people of the past speak through a device called prosopopoeia.

Cicero, in his first *Catiline,* makes the republic speak and Plato, in the prosopopoeia of the *Crito,* shows how Socrates refuses to escape, out of respect for the laws that condemn him. Historical dramas have much of the same power, and it can at least be said for them that they would attract few people if the characters of the past were not given some sort of new life in the plays. *Catiline,* a Roman tragedy by Jonson, may be studied from that point of view, and those who go to Shakespeare's or Corneille's Roman plays are well aware that the accuracy of the author's knowledge matters less than the breath of life that sweeps away the dust of centuries.

The poets know that whether their fame will endure will depend on whether their verse has permanent meaning, but I am not concerned here with the lasting value of a poem. "Immortality", when speaking of poets, is a vague word, and it is worst interpreted in thinking that what is written is fixed for ever. I should like to emphasize the movement, the power of renewal. Spenser, also author of a prosopopoeia,[4] explains what I mean in the following quotation from *Ruines of Rome: by Bellay*[5]

> Bellay (. . .)
> That long hast traveled by thy learned writs,
>   Olde Rome out of her ashes to revive,
> And give a second life to dead decayes:

[4] *Prosopopoeia or Mother Hubberds Tale.*
[5] From "L'Envoy." Both poems are included in the volume of *Complaints.*

Needes must he all eternitie survive,
That can to other give eternall dayes.

That second life may serve as a distinction between literary and everyday reality. I have perhaps sufficiently insisted upon this essential difference, although, since our attention is focused upon the fact of resurrection through the Word, we are led to a more radical distinction. It is not a mere formal difference, it is a difference in origin, nature and kind. I am not trying to eradicate any common sense concept of reality, I suggest only that too little account is taken of the autonomous, original, authentic, valuable and indispensable qualities of literary reality. They require a new life, a new person—whom I call the transcendental person—and what they produce is a radically new, unexisting, unheard of, unsuspected reality in place of the worn-out, existing but unreal, palpable but mortal, exciting but deceiving, established, given, inhuman, unsubstantial reality.

This concept of creative reality is embodied in all great works : but only a writer who feels that the one justification of his life and work lies in creating will be able to tell us what this creative person and reality is.

No one has more systematically inquired into the redemptive properties of literature than Proust, who placed his major work, *A la Recherche du Temps perdu,* under the sign of resurrection, not of a possible, theoretical re-birth, a matter of belief, but an actual, evident one. The last volume, *Le Temps retrouvé,* discloses more than I can explain here. The essential discovery of Proust is the birth of a magnificent work out of the dead past, how the memory of a misused past can be reanimated by the taste of a madeleine.

Proust has been wrongly called a mystic. An exact study of his statements in *Le Temps retrouvé,* and of what he has produced in the earlier books would show that, like many writers and artists, he was preoccupied with the value and justification of artistic truth.

It is significant that Charlotte Haldane, who has written an excellent book on Proust[6], should have devoted a whole chapter, the last one, to this fact of resurrection. I shall quote some extracts from her own translation, in which Proust analyses, not so much his own literary experience, as the universal creative process.

Such a process is impossible without a dissociation from what is called everyday reality:

> "And at once the vicissitudes of life had become indifferent to me, its disasters innocuous, its brevity illusory—this sensation having on me the effect which love has, of filling me with a precious essence; or rather the essence was not in me, it was myself."[7]

Everyday reality is insignificant and empty; from dissatisfaction with this emptiness comes the creative impulse:

> "Seek? More than that: create. It is face to face with something which does not so far exist, to which it alone can give reality and substance, which it alone can bring into the light of day."[8]

It may be argued that this is an exceptional statement. It is, but it applies to the very creative necessity. It would not be so universal, were it not the origin of the novelist's concrete achievement:

> "And just as the Japanese amuse themselves by filling a porcelain bowl with water, and steeping in it little crumbs of paper which until then are without character and form, but, the moment they become wet, stretch themselves and bend, take a colour and distinctive shape . . . so in that

Marcel Proust, London, Arthur Barker Ltd., 1951.
[7] op. cit. p. 122.
[8] ibidem; from *Swann's Way*, Vol. I, pp. 58 et seq.

moment all the flowers in our garden and in M. Swann's park, and the water-lilies on the Vivonne and the good folk of the village and their little dwellings and the parish church and the whole of Combray and of its surroundings, taking their proper shapes and growing solid, sprang into being, town and gardens alike, from my cup of tea."[9]

The cup of tea, rather than a concrete object, is the pre-text from which memories of a lost, virtual self arise. What I have until now called the transcendental self, can be safely identified with the object of the following analysis :

"The person who came to my rescue, who saved me from barrenness of spirit, was the same who, years before, in a moment of identical distress and loneliness, in a moment when I was no longer in any way myself, had come in, and had restored me to myself, for that person was myself and more than myself (the container that is greater than the contents, which it was bringing to me). I had just per-ceived, in my memory, bending over my weariness, the tender, preoccupied, dejected face of my grandmother, as she had been on that first evening of our arrival, the face not of that grandmother whom I was astonished—and re-proached myself—to find that I regretted so little and who was no more of her than just her name, but of my own true grandmother, of whom, for the first time since that after-noon in the Champs-Elysées on which she had had her stroke, I now recaptured, by an instinctive and complete act of recollection, the living reality. That reality has no existence for us so long as it has not been created anew by our mind (otherwise the men who have been engaged in a Titanic conflict would all of them be great epic poets)."[10]

The transcendental person is hidden and secret; created reality, which does not exist, has to be created, not from the

[9] ibidem, p. 124; from *Swann's Way,* Vol. I, p. 62.
[10] ibidem, p. 118 : from *Cities of the Plain,* Vol. I, p. 217.

emptiness that characterizes ordinary reality, but from the whole timeless man sleeping through the accidents of life :

"Of a truth, the being within me, which sensed this impression, sensed what it had in common in former days and now, sensed its extra-temporal character, a being which only appeared, when through the medium of the identity of past and present, it found itself in the only setting in which, it could exist and enjoy the essence of things, that is, outside Time. That explained why my apprehensions on the subject of my death had ceased from the moment when I had unconsciously recognised the taste of the little madeleine, because at that moment the being that I had then been, was an extra-temporal being, and in consequence, indifferent to the vicissitudes of the future. That being had never come to me, had never manifested itself, except when I was inactive and in a sphere beyond the enjoyment of the moment, that was my prevailing condition every time that analogical miracle had enabled me to escape from the present. Only that being had the power of enabling me to recapture former days, Time Lost, in the face of which all the efforts of my memory and my intelligence came to nought."[11]

This is why talent, success, material conditions, will, memory and intelligence will never explain the exceptional genius, for the creative impulse springs from another man, or rather a new man after the old, suffering, lost individual has been abandoned :

"I said to myself : Not only is there still time, but am I in a fit state to accomplish my task? Like a severe spiritual director, my illness had compelled me to renounce the world; but in doing so, it had also done me a service (for if the grain of wheat does not die after it has been sown, it will remain solitary, but if it does die, it will bear many fruits) . . ."[12]

[11] ibidem, p. 133; from *Time Regained,* pp. 212 et seq.
[12] ibidem, p. 136; from the end of *Time Regained.*

A comparison with Christian tradition, and its teaching that the old man must die, that we must be lost in order to be found, is inevitable here. But it would be wrong to attribute the passage quoted above to the Christian tradition. Proust has in mind his own unique experience, representative, not of a doctrine, but of the condition of any creative man. The lost man, and, with him, his memories, is not found by anyone else but himself. Instead of identifying himself with a priest, a mystic or a philosopher because they revere, feel and contemplate a given, divine reality, he identifies himself with the one who gives the till then unexisting reality, with the creative writer :

> "If I thought that Bergotte had spoken falsely when he referred to the joys of spiritual life, it was because I then gave the name of spiritual life to logical reasonings which had no relation with what now existed in me—just as I found society and life wearisome because I was judging them from memories without Truth, whilst now that a true moment of the past had been born again in me three separate times, I had such a desire to live."[13]

It may be objected that I do not sufficiently take account of Proust's conception of time, which is outside the scope of the present study, or that my interpretation as any interpretation must be, is rather free. The text speaks for itself, it is Proust's own unique experience, but it cannot be dismissed as a rare and strange exception. Genius, creation and masterpieces are exceptional, and in this case Proust's analysis applies to a very significant, though exceptional, universal fact : the fact of a second life, of creation compensating for the emptiness left by suffering, the fact of resurrection.

[13] ibidem, p. 134.

22. TRANSFIGURATION

SUCH a phenomenon as resurrection cannot happen without a change. I do not here mean mere transposition, things seen being described in words, or ideas appearing in the form of a character : these are purely technical questions. I mean that the unredeemed, crude reality is transformed through the creative process, through its resurrection, into a personal reality. This is what I have called the ambivalence of literature. That reality is not mere statement, but the statement and the person who makes it and is the conscience of the subject of reality. That person, being the consciousness or the subject, that is, the eye, gives reality what by nature it has not : a face. Through the process of becoming personal, reality is also transfigured. Not transmuted, for you cannot change the nature, the essence of what is. Transfigured so as to suit the subject. A masterpiece is a relation in which the face of things corresponds to the eye.

Creation in literature is not creation out of nothing; resurrection is a rebirth, a new birth from the old being, and so is transfiguration : the new, appropriate face of reality; not a mere mask, for there is something behind, something given, something *a priori,* out of which the complete reality is created. And yet it would be wrong to suppose that what is behind the face is crude reality, for crude reality has no face, or rather it can take any mask we like and remain wholly indifferent to the way in which we look at it.

Transfiguration means here the indissoluble unity of the face and of the eye. As I have to use very abstract terms, it might be convenient to transfer the discussion to more concrete though perhaps vaguer ground. We have all experienced the feeling of our impotence, the impression that the world pays no attention to our desires and does not care what we think of it. Some (the "Weltverbesserer" or "arregla mundos") plan reforms, some suppose that, although the world is not what it should be or what they would like it to be, it is better not to change it, for fear worse should come. I do not intend to attack those writers who advocate a reform, the revolutionists, still less those who bring a spiritual message, but I maintain that it is a secondary task for them. If it had been nothing more than his jokes and his socialism, Bernard Shaw would not be remembered.[1] Ideas and moods are nothing unless they really apply to something; and when they apply, reality cannot be distinguished from them, for it owes its existence to the person who lives in it and through it.

All this is very important, for the writer's task is at stake. Most people believe that the writer's task is to show what the world is and what it should be. Bernard Shaw is no exception; in a plea for didactic literature, he writes of Shakespeare : "He could see no sort of sense in living at all; and Dickens saved himself from the despair of the dream in the Chimes by taking the world for granted and busying himself with its details." Further : "He must be judged by those characters into which he puts what he knows of himself, his Hamlets and Macbeths and Lears and Prosperos. If these characters are agonizing in a void about factitious melodramatic murders and revenges and the like, whilst the comic characters walk with their feet on solid ground, vividly and amusing, you know that the author has much to shew and nothing to teach."[2] Few readers will admit that Shaw does justice to Shakespeare,

[1] This opinion is held by Desmond MacCarthy in his *Shaw*, London, MacGibbon and Kee, 1951, p. 64 : "He has written plays and books that will be read and acted years hence. But he is a philosopher, and he preaches incessantly, with vehemence, theories of right and wrong, about the values of things, and social reform, which are very much open to question."

[2] *Man and Superman,* Epistle Dedicatory, Penguin Books, 563, 1946, XXII.

because in his passion for "effectiveness of assertion" and "Radical opinions" he misses the obvious fact that Shakespeare's characters are living, that they are real, not of an ordinary or artificial reality, but of a transfigured reality. Didacticism can hardly produce that reality, for transfigured reality is not what is or what should be, it is what is felt, experienced, conceived, grasped and realized : the face united with the eye.

The writers' task is not to teach or to reform, it is to create and to transfigure. They are not concerned with the world as it is or as it should be, but as they see it. Whether they really see it or whether they see it in the right way is another question. All writers are, in a way, revolutionists, not because they profess radical opinions, but because the face of their world has some hideous features. They cannot change the world, but, what is much more important, they can transfigure it, make it smile or sneer at their command. They can make it a home for human persons to live in.

23. DISFIGURATION

WHEN a man cannot act, he makes gestures; when he cannot make gestures, he has a secret attitude, and when he cannot keep his attitude secret, he explodes in a fit of creation. Actions, gestures, attitudes and works of art are a human reaction to what is inhuman : events, dumb silent nature, and material power. A necessary reaction, for when man is present he makes his environment human; his essence is to make himself and, by making himself, to make the world. A leaf of grass does so much, but man's activity is of another kind : where he is apparently least active and concrete, powerful and efficient, is where he intervenes best : he is most present in the invisible burst of his mind. Those who smile at Voltaire's light wit avoid seeing that it is not a bodkin, but a sword.

When a writer makes gestures, he is already deprived of his creative power, and when he acts for the sake of a solid cause, party or institution, he has lost his grip on reality, and the creative, personal spirit has left him. Attitudes, opinions, views and beliefs, when they can be detached from the context, mark the mouthpiece, the uncreative writer, and limit him. This tendency culminates in hostile gestures, those of a Claudel or of an Aragon, and ends in iron servitude. The present time is full of such attitudes, gestures and servility; a writer may be characterized as a Communist (Aragon) or a Catholic (Claudel, Péguy, Newman), and these labels are a great help to understanding his works. Indeed, we could hardly find a writer who does not fall into one or other of the present-day categories. My purpose is not to attack such writers, for I should at the same time destroy myself : it is to show that this tendency to outward activity and disintegration is in the end undermined and replaced by a fertile creative period. After the attitudes, the gestures and the obedience to a cause, man must again create and be himself. What all impure writers have in common is that they defend or attack something that exists, something they have not created, something consequently they are not responsible for. I have quoted the names of a French Communist and of an English Catholic who were admittedly defending their cause and attacking the opposition. In this they were none the less narrowly partisan.

For those whose literary merit consists in attacking or defending, transfiguration cannot be anything but a lie, a painted wall. The decoration may be admirable and attractive : when you scratch it, you find the wall. The man perhaps is behind the wall, but you are presented with the wall and cannot see the man.

Much of the art and literature of the twentieth-century is a fake. We now smile more freely at Bernard Shaw's pose as a socialist; the wall is not too hard : it is made of such contradictory materials as paper and fire; but still, the wall offends the eye, more than the eye : the sheer presence of the man is blurred and reality is correspondingly killed by theory. Yet we should not despair. The wall of hell and heaven erected in the Middle Ages was more oppressive than anything we have. Better ridiculous opinions than dogmas. Those who praise the mediæval spirit of obedience and community of thought might well consider two facts : first that no single genius is great because of being mediæval, secondly that the human reality of those times remains a mystery, a prehistorical mystery, for us. What they call obedience is nothing but the absence and oppression of will. So let us keep our picture of the dark Middle Ages. But the stone was piled high, and the wall was painted in vivid, terrifying colours. In a high grade of civilization, the eye reaches beyond the walls and gives a human, divine face to the unattainable reality instead of leaving alone behind the wall things as they are not. All sorts of superstitions, prejudices and more or less spiritual revelations isolate us from reality, but in spite of its many-sidedness and its elusive character, reality wears a unique, human face that appears only to a human presence.

When we say that, in literature, we are looking for what people felt or thought, I suppose that we want at the same time to conjure up the face, the expression of those people, to have them live before us or to feel their presence. What do we know about what people really felt in the Middle Ages? Should we take the *fabliaux,* the mysteries, the lays or the *exempla* seriously? The official face hides the real one, and we must be satisfied either with gaudy but gratuitous satire or with the ideal of chivalry. The people are hardly ever made real; they must have suffered excessively; but the mask of what they were allowed to express is brilliant. And it should not be forgotten that the vigorous popular literature originated in the complete night of oppression.

24. FREEDOM

It follows that the link between creative literature and freedom is obvious. The clerks of the dark ages were busy copying, interpreting, commenting and endlessly glossing. Even in the most brilliant periods, the writers' base praises of their monarch estrange them from us. Racine may be tedious. But freedom must be understood here in a wide sense : neither simply individual freedom nor a social freedom identified with liberal principles, if there are such things. Freedom is above all an idea which, like all ideas, is destroyed by events when it is put into practice. Like other ideas, too, freedom has from time to time an active influence. I am concerned with the second aspect for freedom as a pure theory can be analysed and defined because it is already dead : it is another wall. As a living force, on the contrary, freedom cannot be defined or treated as an abstraction. It becomes the *raison d'être*. This essential freedom through which life becomes a creative act is the bugbear of all established, paralysed régimes, and hardly allows any conformism. As it is one of the indispensable elements of creative writing, it should be possible to show its traces in any work of lasting value. To illustrate my meaning, I shall consider that *Don Quixote,* for example, is a work of freedom, not as a liberation from the novels of chivalry, but as the creation of a representative type of people as they choose to be, and the freedom of *Paradise Lost* lies not in its Puritan or heterodox theology, but in the fact that Milton makes that theology his own. It is true that freedom is often defined as a reaction against oppression, a proof that it is easier to state what liberty is not, than what it is.[1] Yet at least one positive statement can be made : that freedom finds its fulfilment in created life and, by way of consequence, in literature, as opposed to given life. I must repeat here that the difference between created and given life is a difference in kind or in aspect. The created world has a face because it is the product of an eye : the given world exists on its own, whatever we may think of it, suffer from it, feel about it. It is the same world; the difference is that the created world is real (in the special sense given to reality in this book); the given world simply exists and is lost to us for lack of meaning.

The literature of revolt and opposition is not necessarily free, because it often springs from a fixed set of convictions. The communist writers in western countries, for example, must obey rules; this is what they call revolution. The genius, who cannot be confined to such rules, is more than oppressed, he is suppressed.

The shortest definition of creative freedom is that it does not consist in an act or in prompting to action, but lies in a look. The way of seeing is much more important than all activities combined, for it is their origin and their end. A totalitarian régime both imposes its views and forces people to work without asking the meaning of their toil. People, however, can live without butter, not without meaning; their life is a constant search for a meaning. This deep need explains the untimely but lasting, success of those works that propose a meaning, not a system, like St. Augustine's *City of God*, but a way of looking at things, of transfiguring them, that gives them a dazzling meaning. The novels of C. F. Ramaz are a perfect example of such freedom. There is no foreign body of ideas, speculation, philosophy, politics or æsthetics in his novels. There is nothing revolutionary in the

[1] What the judges condemned in Socrates, in Flaubert's *Madame Bovary*, in Baudelaire and in Oscar Wilde, was what they called immorality. But genius, with its essential freedom, is what really offended them.

choice of his characters (most of them vine-growers and the
people of Alpine villages) or in the lives, feelings and actions
of his characters (most of them silent people in a mute landscape). His subject-matter is representative to the point of
banality, and yet he seriously offended his readers. Now he has
been almost universally recognized, and, even in his own
region, they are now forced to accept him, but they cannot
understand him. They easily understand his subject matter,
but his way of dealing with those rude characters is dangerous,
frightful, original, more than revolutionary. He dazzles people,
and they turn their eyes away from the sun to the shadowy,
comfortable banality. The writer's eye burns and transfigures
these common, recognizable characters into reality.

The greatest power of the artist, his dazzling weapon, is the
freedom he is allowed to take with what becomes his landscapes, his characters and his ideas; it is the meaning that he
gives to an otherwise unformed, uncreated, meaningless
existence.

THERE may be, as I also maintain, two kinds of reality, the existing and the created, but ultimately there is only one. There is no uncreated, meaningless reality. As soon as you think of something, you begin to create that something and you are in a way responsible for it. Imagine that someone assumes responsibility for a world, even for a limited, one-sided world! That small world will have more effect on the future than all visible and invisible events. If you want to destroy that small world, you must be stronger than the man who made it; and you can be stronger, for you are free, quite free, excessively free. If you ever realize how free you are you will look round for something to hold on to, for you are freer than the eagle; around you there is nothing but emptiness, you have to make something out of it, either a comfortable repetition of platitudes, work and sleep, life and death, or a dazzling meaning. You may be bored to death, for there is nothing, no reality and no meaning, only the effort : not the daily, but the eternal, free effort of creating both reality and meaning.

It does not follow that there are no given facts or that reality is pure invention. Here we touch the pivot of the world and of its image, our philosophy of literature. As I have already stated, we do not create out of nothing, nor can we represent the world as it is. Nothingness and facts are the two opposite and extreme temptations. A novel of pure imagination would be a monster, so also would a novel made of statistics. Facts are already dead; nothingness is not yet born. Reality lies between, in assimilated facts and in controlled imagination. Readers are perverse and subject to the whims of fashion, but they are all and always curious about one thing, one thing they are too weak or lazy to provide for themselves : reality. Few of them understand that reality is meaning, that is, a relation, all the same meaning is what they are looking for, what kindles their thirst.

LET us consider a special kind of freedom : that of the novelist when, instead of drawing on his memories or on any documents, he has to imagine and present something he has never seen, never experienced, never heard of. This may seem an extreme case, for it is often argued that all novels are autobiographical. But I say that this situation is not only common, but also inescapable if the novel is to have a meaning at all. Let us suppose that you have imagined a character who commits suicide. You are not obliged to present a clinical diagnosis of his motives, but you must at least suggest why he takes his decision, and show the inescapable trend of circumstances and reactions towards the act. The act itself must have a meaning and it can be isolated, provided that it remains in harmony with the rest of the novel. This is the law of art : all the details must live in harmony, or there is no meaning. Your aim is clear : to show the artistic necessity of a suicide.

Now artistic necessity means neither explanation nor justification. The artistic law of unity allows so much freedom that you are perplexed. You may think of a relative of yours who committed suicide, and of the motives which may have prompted him to that decision. You knew him well, you have spent years side by side with him in the same office, yet you had no idea that his life was so unlike yours. You could not have foreseen it. Do you know yourself? Impossible, life is not so reduced to rule !

You may think also of Medea and Cleopatra. Their suicides are wonderfully logical. But these are literary suicides. Your character must be as consistent as Euripides' Medea or

Shakespeare's Cleopatra, but you know that your relative who committed suicide was not consistent, otherwise you would have foreseen his death. You are not consistent; with an effort you can struggle against your nature and behave as a stoic, but you cannot foresee how you will feel when you are old. Will you become indifferent and passive, or will you feel the lust and rage that Yeats once sung? Who are you even now? You see that, to give a meaning to your novel and to your character, you must imitate Eripides' and Shakespeare's clarity. To achieve unity, you must create, for all the facts you know about your relative will not make his suicide consistent. You must invent, in order to make a literary suicide. You are more capable of inventing your character than of knowing that nearest to you : yourself.

Why does Goethe's Werther commit suicide, whereas Dostoievsky's characters do not, although they suffer more than Werther? With Goethe, it may have been a need for dismissing somebody he had been, his past self, and perhaps Dostoievsky wanted his characters to suffer as much as he himself did in Siberia. In both cases, at least, the characters are very different from any living person, or, if the author draws them from his own substance, they are one of his thousand possibilities, never the present one. What you are depends on what you have been and on what you will be, so that, ultimately, you have no present being.

The character you create, on the contrary, must appear as a whole, and your novel must be coherent even if your character is not. Your relative may be tall or short. It does not matter, this is one of the thousand possibilities, but if in your novel you choose him to be short, this choice must determine something else in your novel, let us say an inferiority complex which, in turn, becomes one element in your composition. You must and will compose with details drawn from life, from observation, from memories and from imagination, but the mere act of selecting details and of assembling them into an artistic whole makes them utterly different from anything that exists. You cannot select and assemble the details after your whim or without any order. You obey certain laws of composition, comply with the requirements of your instrument, the written word, and achieve unity. If your character's life is a common and boring one, your novel must be anything but common and boring, one more proof that there is a gulf between your character and any existing person, the abyss of your absolute freedom from which a no less absolute necessity will emerge. To be real, your character must be harmoniously presented.

I have now taken my argument far enough to be able to conclude. I have shown, on the one hand the meaninglessness of present life and existing things, on the other hand the possibility of arriving through invention at a meaning. The power or liberty of the novelist is discouragingly absolute. When his note-book is full he has still to start work. Then he starts making use of his freedom but, instead of producing a unity with a meaning he may still fall into the snares of arbitrariness, irrelevancy and whimsicality. Reality is a difficult thing to make, for you must start from absolute freedom, from using your power over existing but meaningless and therefore unreal things, and end at the point where everything in your novel is harmonious, full of meaning and real. It is fiction, but it must be real, unlike life. It presupposes freedom, but leads ultimately to perfect necessity. You have realized that reality is not something that is, or that is given; if it were so, you would have no choice, no invention, no possibilities, no imagination. Reality must be created, made of observed, remembered or imagined details, but selected, transfigured and united into a meaning. This is one of the best services that the study of literature may pay to the philosopher: to show him that reality is not, but must be invented or made, and to invite him to look for it in literature as well as in science.

PART THREE

In the Open Heart

27. SOME PLANNING

I AM aware that my philosophy of literature is not quite methodical. The logical links between the parts are sometimes hidden, sometimes loose. My task, however, is not to build different materials after a pre-established plan, but to use the same materials throughout the work so as to show both their inner structure and their several aspects. These two different aims determine the first two parts.

A rigid composition was undesirable, for it would have broken up an essentially whole reality into fragments. Like the plot of a novel, however, a certain method is the thread of my book. For many readers the argument may perhaps seem less exciting than the plot of a novel, but I hope they will grow more interested as they observe that my apparently aimless path is leading somewhere. At the present stage of the book their curiosity may urge them to ask three questions: where do we come from, where are we and where are we going to?

To the first of these questions I answer that, in the first part, I have endeavoured to derive a philosophy (more specifically an ontology) from a view of literary reality and from reality itself. The second part exhibits rather[1] the reverse trend:

[1] I say "rather," for I have used by-ways and short-cuts.

starting from the philosophy that arises from literary reality, I have tried to build up a view of literature and as, in this case, the view and the thing are identical, I have been concerned with some aspects of what I call—and make—literary.

Where are we, then? The conclusion of each of the first two parts can be summed up in a few words. In the first part, emphasizing both the unity and the ambivalence of literature, I have come to the philosophical conclusion that reality, far from being an objective entity, depends on our own understanding, and correspondingly that meaning, the essence of literature, consists in the harmonious relation between the things constituting reality and their effects on our soul. The second part leads to the simple conclusion that reality, and here I mean literary reality as well as any other kind of reality, has to be made; in the first part I had to assume the existence of the finished work, and to postpone the study of the creative process in order to derive an ontological knowledge; the second part is devoted to the making of literature.

I may now put forward an answer to the third question. The third part will have two starting points, namely the two conclusions we have arrived at. There remains for me the task of deciding on my aim. The two conclusions mentioned above seem at first to have nothing in common, for they result from investigations undertaken in two contrary directions, the first originating in the works as end-products, the second pointing to literary reality as a creative, never completed process. If these opposite directions are not to lead to a contradiction, we have to effect a synthesis of both results. My aim in the third part will be to show how the creative process described in the second part unites external reality with our own perceptions, and how such harmony is fulfilled in a few selected passages.

The aim of the third part is neither to extract a philosophy nor to analyse the creative process. This time I shall let the works speak and, as they have to be continuously created, I shall contribute my modest and intrusive, but indispensable interpretation. I do not claim to make any new discovery in the field of criticism, but I shall try to throw a new light on works already known. This attitude, even if my attempts at interpretation fail, justifies me and may tempt a better pen to the task, for literature is not only what many authors have written, but above all what every one makes of it, the one who reads and the one who does not.

To sum up the three parts in one sentence : I have laid the foundation for an understanding of reality, then I have described literature in the making, and now, as in this case the understanding and the making amount to the same thing, I do both at the same time, to see how far theory and action may agree.

28. EFFECT IN DRAMA

In our search for a synthesis we may remember one of the remarks on poetry at the end of Part One : that poetry admits neither the primacy of skill nor the primacy of subject-matter. Now, poetry, though apparently simple, is the most synthetic of all arts, and the difference between mediocrity and excellence is so tiny—though important—is the movement of such a delicate balance that most readers are unaware of it, or if they feel it they declare, as many critics do, that they are unable to analyse it. You can analyse your feelings as a reader, the effects of poems on other readers, the meaning of the poet, the means through which he produces such effects, etc., but to describe the harmony, the synthesis, lies perhaps beyond human powers.

Because it is more composite, drama is a much less synthetic form of expression than poetry, and some of its elements can be isolated without damage. Although poetry and drama are fundamentally the same, a way of giving life a meaning (what a daring, creative, almost impossible undertaking!) yet in poetry everything must be integrated into the substance of words, whereas in drama much is left to the actors, the scenery, the audience, etc.

The necessary tricks of the theatre find little use in poetry, where the author relies entirely upon individual appreciation. Everything must be harmonious, and the harmony of the whole is so coherent that it is impossible to describe it. Some elements are sometimes analysed, among them rhyme, rhythm, alliteration, assonance, music, composition, etc., and a magic effect is ascribed to them. The magic of the poets is like the gods of the theologians : they rely on it because they live on it, knowing that, in itself, it is nothing but lies and emptiness, like Mallarmé's murmuring shell :

Aboli bibelot d'inanités sonores.

Primitive people had to use such tricks, which may have both exerted a power and given a meaning to life, both of which are lost to us. We are what we are now, and the poet must either relax his grip on reality or use other means. Prosody and scansion have become conscious. They are a foreign body within poetry, mere versification, music added to the meaning, not integrated into it, and those who rely on such means in order to impress their meaning or to convince cannot be sincere if sincerity implies coherence. Modern poets encounter such extraordinary difficulties in collecting themselves and imposing harmony and meaning upon their and our chaotic life, that superstition and magic can only prevent them from coping with their task, and make the world still more uncontrollable, strange and frightful than it is.

Compared to poetry, drama is composite. You cannot judge the effect of a play before you have seen it played, and then much depends on the theatre, the stage-manager, the actors, the scenery, the audience, etc. Some of the component parts can be distinctly isolated, so that it is possible to determine what the synthesis consists of. I should like to draw attention to two significant component parts : the sympathy or disapproval inevitably aroused in the public by the characters. These moral attitudes, in all their variety, stand outside the play, except when the actors directly addresses the audience; they are not expressed in words, and yet they cling to the characters, whatever they may say or do. The audience is invited to participate and is rarely indifferent. Now it is useful to distinguish, among the various attitudes of the audience, two fundamental ones : identification (sympathy) and condemnation (antipathy). It is well known that the audience invariably identifies itself with the 'good' characters, so that ethical and social values cannot be dismissed from the theatre. These phenomena of identification and condemnation also attach to the characters of a novel, but less vividly, less distinctly; it is no essential requisite of a novel that the readers should feel attraction or repulsion for the characters. On the stage, however, the audience is there, the character is there with a human face or with a mask, with words and actions, and the phenomena of attraction and repulsion occur directly between them. This interplay between actors and spectators is by no means contained in the written play. Let us examine it objectively, that is, neither from the spectator's nor the character's point of view. The first remark is that it is not sufficient for the characters to act and to suffer, to laugh and to weep; they must either judge themselves or be judged; this makes the whole difference between a comic character, who makes us laugh and judges the others on condition that we sympathize with him, and a ridiculous one, whom we judge and whom we laugh *at*, not *with*, because we are aware of the extravagance of his conduct. But where is that awareness to be found if it is not expressed? This is assuredly one of the most remarkable features of the theatre, that it is capable of creating or arousing the collective consciousness of the audience. Certain plays startle us, trouble us, and arouse feelings that were dormant or that we had never experienced. The plays that satisfy us most are those that produce that effect most acutely, through which the author speaks directly to the soul, across the written words, across the stage setting, across the actors, but not to impose his own views, distort the truth and mislead our unerring judgment, for the awareness he has created is neither his nor ours, it is a sense of communion.

This fact shows how one of the apparently external elements of the drama contributes to the unity of the play and becomes a factor in the composite harmony of drama. It shows also what unpredictable and invisible materials the playwright works with. The lowest scoundrel on the stage and the least serious of actions may produce a deep effect and elevate us as much as the most saintly hero, on condition . . . On condition that they are true, of course; this looks obvious enough. Othello is as true as Desdemona. But what is truth in the theatre, how can we say that one character is true, another not? We do not know ourselves, even though we pretend to know others well, for we seldom reach the bottom of our weakness or the height of our worthiness; we know ourselves as we are in ordinary circumstances, everyday, we know our past and our ambitions, yet this is only the thousandth part of our possibilties, a fraction of our whole being. What power is that of the playwright who can thus reveal something of the truth about us? That truth is neither in the character's mouth nor in us; it is an invisible reality created by the play that moves us, and we recognize it immediately. A character may make us weep, his fate may seem cruel to us, and even insensitive people will cry, but our sympathy and reprobation have their laws: we cannot grant our sympathy to an unworthy character. Plays are truly tragic or truly comic, not according to the taste of the moment and of a particular audience, they are always and immediately so.

We have now considered a new aspect of literary reality: its effect. This brings us one step forward, for we are compelled to search for that reality not only in the works themselves, but also in our own reactions. Reality and our own understanding of reality are one and the same thing. As the undefinable, invisible spirit clings so obstinately to reality, however, we are still faced by the same overwhelming difficulty, for the truth is not so much in our object, the work, as outside. It is in both, and this constitutes another piece of evidence for my contention that meaning—the essence of literature—is a relation, a many-sided relation plunging its roots into our soul and uniting it with the outside world through the drama. If characters have any reality, they acquire it through the eyes of the spectators.

Great works of art, for instance Milton's *Paradise Lost* and Victor Hugo's *Légende des Siècles,* are said to be pervaded with a cosmic sense. The word 'universe' is used instead of 'world'. But what is the universe without an eye to make it real, what is life without awareness? The conclusion of the first part of the present book is that reality is inseparable from the perception of reality, and now we see that the relation is established not only between the object and the subject, but also, plunging its roots within our soul, between the object, its representation through the work of art, and the subject. I may as well add another extension of the relation, invisible like the preceding one : the creative mind of the writer. The second part of this book adds the conclusion that reality is not what exists, but what is made, so that, when reality is created in literature, reality distinctly bears the imprint of the writer's personality.

All these things constitute reality : the writer's person, his object, the representation of his object through his work, and the effect of his work on the readers or the audience, though not so much these things separately or together as their harmonious relations. When each of these component parts is in its proper place, then we have something more than reality, then we have attained truth, to use this word for the second time in this book.

The word 'truth' often denotes something, sharp, hard, strong and irrefutable. It should not be forgotten that truth is at the same time a vaporous thing : as we have seen, two at least of its component parts are invisible : the subject and the effect; they are more than invisible, they are the seeing elements. And yet truth is hard and incisive, striking the spectators of a play as relentlessly as the vicious characters, however much the audience may sympathize only with the virtuous characters. A truth that castigates us is, once more, neither the character's nor the spectator's, nor even quite the author's truth, though each of them contributes to it in its own way; it is above them and inside them, it is the severe, unwritten law at which the writer's creative freedom has aimed, the binding fraternal law of meaning, and the happy smiling law of harmony. The actors weep and laugh, but the spectators do not always weep when the actors weep, they sometimes laugh at the actor's tears, and weep at his laughter. There is a law that commands such attractions and repulsions, for they are unlike our usual arbitrary reactions towards existing people, whom we judge more according to our interests and wishes than according to their merits. The characters of a play become the perfect objects of our feelings, and indeed their truth is partly made up of the correspondence between their being and our feelings (their effects), as well as between their being, the writer's personality and the persons they are supposed to represent. Truth belongs to none of these four kinds of component, but it is what unites them. This statement both corroborates and enlightens our concept of meaning as a relation and of reality as neither of things nor of ideas. We now see that truth extends its roots as far in the soul as reality reaches into the invisible recesses of matter, and we may confidently suppose that it is not to be found in either of them, but in their harmony.

K

29. TRUTH AND REALITIES IN *Wuthering Heights*

As truth is no more in the soul than reality is in matter, we are justified in looking for them in what, in achieving harmony, creates them, in literature, provided that we keep in mind the invisible character of that truth. For though, in the first part of this book I have advocated the reality of fictitious characters, I now realize that their reality is not in themselves, but in the correspondence or contrast between themselves and their effects upon us, without forgetting their correspondence with the existing persons they represent and with the person of the author.

Real characters (in the sense given to that word in the first part of this book) thus provoke a deep resonance which is as much part of the book or of the play, though an invisible, unexpressed part, as their fictitious being. In the light of this consideration we shall study a passage from Emily Brontë's *Wuthering Heights*, where a character whose reality can hardly be contested expresses her feelings. The reader should be reminded that Catherine, who married Linton during Heathcliff's absence, is devoured by her love for Heathcliff, her father's adopted son. I simply quote this passage, for my task is not to show what the character's feelings are or how they are made manifest; all this is so wonderfully expressed, so evident, that I may leave the text to speak for itself and refer the reader to the context. My task is rather to find what is less evident, what I called the invisible, the seeing parts of truth. Here is the passage in which Catherine addresses Mrs. Dean, her cook who has just told her of Linton's behaviour :

' "Among his books!" she cried, confounded. "And I dying! I on the brink of the grave! My God! does he know how I'm altered?" continued she, starting at her reflection in a mirror hanging against the opposite wall. "Is that Catherine Linton! He imagines me in a pet—in play, perhaps. Cannot you inform him that it is frightful earnest? Nelly, if it be not too late, as soon as I learn how he feels, I'll chose between these two; either to starve at once—that would be no punishment unless he had a heart—or to recover and leave the country. Are you speaking the truth about him now? Take care. Is he actually so indifferent for my life?" '

Now a woman reader may unconditionally sympathize with Catherine and endorse her preference of Heathcliff, a rich, outcast, but full-blooded gypsy, to the quiet and kind Linton whose love is lukewarm. So much sympathy, however, would be checked in the course of the novel, at least by Mrs. Dean's commonsense, for Catherine is a tragic character; we pity her, but she alone bears the responsibility for her loss. Mrs. Dean is supposed, with little likelihood, to relate a great part of the story, and at the same time of the crisis from which our episode is taken, her weatherproof firmness appears as a relaxation from the utmost tension sustained throughout the novel. Besides, her humble position prevents her from intervening except by acting as a moderator between the thwarted loves and unchained hatred of her masters. Another reason for her impartial attitude as a narrator is that she speaks of a person who has died. She understands Catherine as she understands Heathcliffe. Because she has nursed him, she cannot share Isabella's (Catherine's sister-in-law) hatred for Heathcliff, but at the same time she understands that hatred.

After these explanations it is clear that the reader is not invited to hate some characters and to identify himself with others. He will rather feel and understand Catherine's love for Heathcliff as well as Isabella's hatred, for the truth of these characters is made of the following realities :

1.—Emily Brontë's characters, so far as they bear the imprint of her personality, so far as they are autobiographical, are part of herself, are seen through her eyes, are presented in her own way and express themselves through her own words. This reality is evident in our passage, for though Catherine is supposed to speak and uses colloquial forms, her style is too literary, her behaviour too threatrical to conceal the author's hand.

2.—Her models, or the persons they are supposed to represent. Emily Brontë died in 1848 when she was thirty; she is labelled 'Victorian', though romantic imagination and the love of the Yorkshire moors are more apparent in the novel than exact observation and experience of social life and individual characters.[1] She displays very little of Trollope's Victorian realism, a realism confined to ordinary people of the middle classes, informed by a wide experience and animated by patient methodical work[2], not by flashes of genius and unique inspiration as is *Wuthering Heights*.

In spite of all this, Emily Brontë's characters are highly

[1] " . . Pater seized on *Wuthering Heights,* in preference to any work of Scott's, as the 'really characteristic fruit' of the spirit of romanticism. That only proves once more the inadequacy of these outworn shibboleths, since from another point of view *Wuthering Heights,* with its unerring unity of conception and its full catharsis of the emotions of pity and terror, is one of the very few occasions on which the novel has reached the dignity of classical tragedy." Herbert Read, *Collected Essays in Literary Criticism,* London, Faber and Faber, 1938, p. 297.

[2] "I had arranged a system of task-work for myself, which I would strongly recommend to those who feel as I have felt, that labour, when not made absolutely obligatory by the circumstances of the hour, should never be allowed to become spasmodic." *Autobiography,* Ch. VII.

representative of a desolate country and endowed with a deep social significance, for she has clearly drawn the consequences of Heathcliff's (the gypsy's) presence in the farm. It is certainly difficult to isolate this second type of reality because the first one is so predominant, a characteristic of the romantics who can hardly detach their characters from themselves, so overwhelming was their sense of *"le moi"*! The landscapes in *Wuthering Heights* have nothing of Lamartine's vagueness;[3] the reader gets the impression that he might go and check the accuracy of the information, and at the same time he sees those details, the two country houses, the moors, the snow, the church; he is haunted by them. The characters too are haunted. Those landscapes, therefore, are objectively true enough, but they remain enveloped in an atmosphere, they are inseparable from their meaning, they are not objectively seen. Here, too, Emily Brontë is unable to detach her creations from her own eyes.

I may conclude that there is an objective reality in *Wuthering Heights,* not very apparent in our passage (Linton's staying among his books is a realistic feature), quite different from Trollope's realism, and yet authentic and reliable. The trouble is that it cannot be freed from the powerful attraction of the author's vision.

3.—The characters as they see themselves. This type of reality is plainly illustrated by our passage, even symbolized by the mirror. For the reader who is inclined to see there the only reality because it is the expressed one, I would point out its narrowness; what Catherine sees in the mirror is the shadow of herself, but, for her, the shadow is real, and all the realities of Thrushcross Grange, the seat of the Lintons, count for nothing; she dwells at Thrushcross Grange, yet she lives at Wuthering Heights; she lives with Linton,

[3] The English romantics, like Rousseau, are capable of reliable, detailed and accurate, even geographical description. I think of Byron and Shelley, and of their influence on the birth of tourism in Switzerland.

yet he is absent from her life; she is haunted by Heathcliff. That shadowy being engendered by herself is so real that she finally becomes it. She becomes spiritually the wife of *her* Heathcliff. She makes herself what she sees herself to be, and kills her self as seen by the others.

4.—The characters as the reader sees them. I have already insisted that Catherine is a tragic character, in order to warn the reader, who has only our passage under his eyes, against wholly identifying himself with Catherine. He may pity her for her husband's desertion and for her illness, but he has also to judge her with a certain detachment. Were she to "leave the country": the reader would condemn her. Our episode stands in the middle of a crisis, just before she goes mad from fever and hysteria.[4] Knowing this, the reader cannot reject her; he is a witness of the strength of character that causes her physical weakness, of the unselfish passion that causes her to sacrifice her duty and her life in the service of a higher justice (Heathcliff is not guilty because he is a gypsy and an outcast). On the whole, the reader is agitated by various conflicting opinions and approaches; 'his' character lives in him. I only want to draw attention to the variety of the reader's feelings. For the rest, he is the best judge of what he feels towards Catherine. Though fictitious, she is real to him.

5.—The characters as they see one another. This is the first time I mention this type of reality. It is one of the evident types of reality, and it is excellently illustrated in our passage. At least we know what Catherine thinks of her husband when she asks, a few lines above:

' "What is that apathetic being doing?" she demanded, pushing her thick entangled locks from her wasted face. "Has he fallen into a lethargy, or is he dead?" '

---

[4] The fit is almost clinically described, an argument speaking against the common assumption, propagated by her sister (see *Biographical Notice* of Ellis and Acton Bell) that she was neither experienced nor learned, and in favour of point 2.

The reality of Catherine's Edgar Linton is so distinct from the reality of the reader's, or the narrator's Edgar Linton that neither the reader nor the narrator, nor probably the author, share Catherine's views, though they admit that Edgar Linton could not appear otherwise in Catherine's eyes.

This type of reality is represented by such variety in *Wuthering Heights,* as in most novels, that I must confine my investigation to Catherine's Edgar Linton. The writing of dramatic dialogue requires such versatility that the author becomes familiar with the relativity of his characters' reality.

30. FUSION AND DISTINCTNESS

IF there is no truth in *Wuthering Heights*, in which we have found so many realities, I wonder where truth is to be discovered. I admit that some of those realities are also inevitably, but not convincingly represented in bad novels. The only reality that I have found it difficult to isolate is the objective reality, which does not stand out distinctly because it is fused into the author's subjective reality; it is none the less extant. The only thing we can say of that type of reality is that it is there; with all the others a mere presence is not sufficient: they must be convincing. Among all the types of reality found in our passage,[1] none is more convincing than the fictitious reality: Catherine as she sees herself. It is also the most evident one, with the dramatic reality (the characters as they see one another) and the artistic reality (the characters as the author sees and makes them). It is a paradox that the objective reality should be, in our passage, the least evident one after the reader's reality. The reader's reality is always invisible and there is no doubt that Catherine is real for the reader. We have seen that she lives both in and outside him.

All these realities, with some others, exist in poetry, where they are so fused together that we cannot see them distinctly or isolate them without violating the harmony. It is significant that the only reality I found it hard to isolate, the objective reality, is precisely the one that is enveloped in a poetic atmosphere.

From the beginning of the novel, after our first visit to Wuthering Heights, we readers are caught in a spell; our

[1] which is far from being representative of the novel in this respect.

curiosity draws us towards that place, and after the second eventful visit we must know. The narrator may quietly begin her story, we are prepared to listen, we are interested in whatever may explain the startling behaviour of those who haunt Wuthering Heights as well as of its living inhabitants. We, for whom the behaviour of relatives, neighbours and foreigners has no secret, are perplexed by Wuthering Heights, and reminded that it is not what we see in other people's conduct that matters; it is what is hidden.

For the reader, therefore, Wuthering Heights is at first a problem to be solved. Thanks to Emily Brontë, the reader is exceptionally willing to understand somebody. Here I leave the reader and come back to the philosopher, who wonders what this spell and this need for understanding are. If I relate them to our series of realities, I observe, as I have already shown, first that the spell, the charm, the atmosphere and the poetry of *Wuthering Heights* come from the clinging together of two realities; in this case the objective and the subjective realities are made one, but others may be added to the indissoluble unity. In poetry, for example, what I called the artistic reality must necessarily fuse itself into another reality. This, rather than versification, is perhaps what makes the difference between poetry and prose. The poet's skill as a versifier is distrusted when it bears no relation to what he has to say; so also the beauty of what the poet says remains ineffective when marred by an awkward form of expression.

Poetry, therefore, is characterized by the fusion of its various realities. Perfect unity, however, has never been attained in a single poem; one or other type of reality remains always distinct from the rest, is not fully integrated, so that impurities, imperfections and a certain degree of artificiality are tolerated. The pure uncompromising truth has not yet been uttered, for the poet will always exclude those implications of his meaning that he is unable to assimilate. For the sake of unity he will commit a sin against wholeness.

Unity, as opposed to mere relation, distinguishes poetry from prose, for prose demands less than poetry. It is easier to attain a certain degree of perfection in prose, where various realities may remain distinct, and yet in harmony with the whole. They need not be fused into one another. Distinctness in prose is even a merit, and poetry is often mistaken for confusion and mistiness. Nevertheless, all these considerations of fusion and distinctness suggest that among all the varieties of meaning there is a progressive scale ranging from mere representation of objects to perfect unity; the degree of harmony is the criterion.

I have refrained from analysing poetry only because I have experienced the danger and vanity of analysing it. Valéry is an appropriate subject for academic study because the subtlest affective shades of his meaning are consciously introduced into his poems; but even there the intellectual scaffolding of the poem cannot be removed or the house will fall. The French interpretation of Poe's *Philosophy of Composition* is interesting but misleading. Method and logic are certainly important, but the power of synthesis, the ability to see the hidden relations of things and to hold various conflicting elements together in order to find their affinities, is more important. We have just seen that when a poet decides to eliminate an element from a poem he does so more from necessity than from virtue; he fails to transform all his raw materials. This is why so many pure poems are one-sided; they impress us very much, though we feel that something is limping and distorted : perfection has been reached at the expense of wholeness. On the reverse, poems more ambitious and all-embracing are impure; there is no distortion, but there is a lack of beauty : completeness has been reached at the expense of perfection.

Whatever may be the balance of merits and defects of a poem, the crowning virtue resides in the harmonious correspondence of its realities, a virtue that cannot be analysed because it consists precisely in indissoluble unity. The meaning of prose is a synthesis and can be analysed, like the 'prosaic' elements of a poem.

I cannot emphasize enough that the whole, the unity, the harmony and the correspondence of meaning matter more than each of the component realities, and that within the whole harmony, each type of reality must be harmonious, for each reality (I mean here, of course, the created reality) is endowed with its proper meaning and therefore implies a correspondence, a requirement which we have, I think, sufficiently considered in the first part of the book.

I have now been led to discover a new sphere of harmony, situated above the mere correspondence and interplay between object and subject, the sphere that contains all the others. It is a generalization of the notion of meaning as relation, which was discussed in the first part, and involves the dynamic process, some aspects of which are shown in the second part. It is living and relative, not fixed and absolute; even poetic perfection is no absolute; far from being a self-sufficient entity, standing outside an imperfect reality, it is a relative balance in which various realities are struggling for equipoise.

WE may ask why so many realities are necessary for the making of truth. Is truth so complicated? The apparent simplicity of a novel is due to the character's individuality and induces many readers to consider exclusively fictitious reality, that is, the character as he sees, feels and expresses himself.

Unlike most readers, who prefer to read without asking questions, the philosopher may also wonder why fictitious reality is at all necessary, why a character must be given a name, an individual place in society and an individual fate, as if he existed. The philosopher may well wonder, for, as a philosopher, he prefers to state and solve problems in general terms, which for him are the only terms, and he would be ashamed of a fictitious problem, the character being necessarily false in his eyes, even as a mere hypothesis.

Who is right, the reader who consents to the familiar suspension of disbelief, or the philosopher who rejects the fiction? Neither of them, if the reader is blind to the merely relative function of the character, and if the philosopher does not recognize the need for creation. Comparing those two attitudes, I should prefer the reader's attitude, for in spite of his blindness, he lives with the character and, by doing so, proves that there is some reality in fiction. The philosopher, on the contrary, restrains his sympathy or his antipathy on the ground that they should not be given to a person who does not exist. Because he refuses to contribute to the reality of that person, he prevents himself from understanding the meaning of the novel. It cannot be argued that no meaning can be found is any novel; consequently the philosopher is wrong in this case, and the invention of fictitious characters is justified.

I am far from arguing that the problems of life cannot be stated in general terms, but I do say that no problem can be solved for ever in a general and absolute way, not even the most abstract ones, the mathematical problems; for after Einstein it is foolish to think that there is nothing relative in a perfect, abstract and theoretical figure of geometry. Even the most elementary of geometrical elements, the point, is a creation and stands in relation to the human mind.

The reader is right when he wants an individual person to be created in order to personify a life, a meaning and a truth, and the philosopher is wrong when he refuses to see any truth derived from a fictitious reality. The philosopher's fallacy is very serious in this case for he does not admit the necessity of a creation. He does not see that reality is not, but is made; this is the core of his blindness.

As an illustration of this fallacy I have chosen Emerson. So far my philosopher has been a general and fictitious invention of my own, I propose to show how such an attitude may be represented by an individual author, one more demonstration that, to be real, any reality must be accepted by a person who is responsible for it. As to 'my' reader, nobody but himself can confirm his reality. I have tried partly to identify myself with him, partly to invent him. I grant that my creature is too philosophically pure and distinct to be true, and I hope that, if he helps a little, he may become real. Philosophical distinctness, however, is another means of conferring individuality and pungency on an idea, another symptom of creation; but here, instead of inventing a concrete fiction as the novelist does, I have built up an abstract hypothesis to be verified by the reader himself. Expressed in abstract terms, this relation appears as follows : my idea of the reader is to be confirmed by the idea the reader forms of himself. What a world of illusions, all trying to come true and all calling for an author !

EMERSON, that great and inexhaustible source of ideas, typifies a fundamental misunderstanding of art. With a few exceptions, *Brahma* for example, his poems are not poetry. He is a preacher and an essayist, and like all preachers he has many realities in his mind, three in particular: everyday reality, the light of truth, and ethics; what men think they are, what men should believe and what men should be. With this trinity alone he could not have understood art. Both his concept of nature and his ethics were too sharply and independently felt for him to understand the essential unity of art. He always looks for something outside the work of art, either truth ('nature') or, as in this passage from his essay on *Art*, ethics: "In the sculptures of the Greeks, in the masonry of the Romans, and in the pictures of the Tuscan and Venetian masters, the highest charm is the universal language they speak. A confession of moral nature, of purity, love, and hope, breathes from them all."[1]

It would be easy to pick out very many still more ridiculous statements in the same essay or elsewhere, but that would be unfair to Emerson. He is constantly off the mark, and yet, in the higher spheres, he touches the reality of art. He does not admit that art can create another reality than his ordinary or natural reality, nor does he notice that his wonderful concepts of nature and of the over-soul[2] are his own invention, his creation, his nature as he makes it. Because he was unable to notice the original freedom of art—his own

[1] From: *The Works of E.*, Volume I, London, Bell, 1883, p. 149.
[2] cf. my notion of the whole man.

revolutionary, dangerous, uncomfortable freedom—he despised and feared works of art as such and placed them as mere accessories, below any useful thing: "When its errands are noble and adequate, a steamboat bridging the Atlantic between Old and New England, and arriving at its port with the punctuality of a planet, is a step of man into harmony with nature. The boat at St. Petersburg, which plies along the Lena by magnetism, needs little to make it sublime. When science is learned in love, and its powers are wielded by love, they will appear the supplements and continuations of the material creation."[3]

Such is the conclusion of an essay on art! What is 'the little' that the boat needs to make it sublime? Perhaps a Joseph Conrad. As to the science learned in love and its powers wielded by love, we know more than Emerson did. Emerson's material creation, wonderful as he sees it, with its decorative supplements and its useful continuation, is a creation of his own; yet he was wise enough to see that pure transcendental spirit and pure matter are the same thing. He was an unconscious artificer.

It should be noted that my criticism is not levelled at Emerson's works, which I admire, but at a misunderstanding and contempt of art typical of a young nation; he values nature higher than culture only because culture is, largely something foreign, whereas nature is his own. But what is culture, if not nature owned and won by the human mind? In this light, nature appears as the mirror of human impotence, as a mere absence of man, as a triumph of barbarism.

It is not surprising that the problem of cultural tradition, of the humanization of matter and nature, and of artistic creation, should appear with acute urgency in American literature. This may justify me in devoting the following chapters to American literature.

[3] ibid., p. 153.

NOTHING is more remarkable than the act of writing, in which you commit your thought to a tiny thread, express your life and capture some reality. A thin piece of paper becomes the realm of the spirit, in which you mark the presence—or the absence—of consciousness in life, winning a round in the struggle against nature.

Printed paper, bridges, roads, electric wires, all the appliances of civilization are inscribed in the voiceless book of nature. Whatever in them belongs to nature will return to oblivion, but the other, the spiritual aspect, remains in man himself.

Violence and selfishness, accumulation and destruction of matter on the one hand, moderation, purposeful open-minded creation on the other hand: man imposing his presence, looking for his spirit in nature, work and art.

The trouble about Emerson's steamboat, the defect that makes it inartistic, is that it consists exclusively of the objective reality and does not care about 'noble and adequate errands'. It is a plain steamboat used for commercial purposes, not as 'a step of man into harmony with nature'. The slave trade was a good business a few centuries ago, and was carried out with only one aim: profit. The danger of mistaking art for morality is evident. Does profit, the mainspring of Western civilization, belong to nature or to man? Whichever it may be, it runs the danger of escaping from man's hands. The steamboat sails towards profit; laws and ethics are subservient to profit, and the passengers may admire the sea if they have time. Such are the disconnected realities of a civilization that is falling to pieces. If man really wants something else than profit, then he has to create a reality other than Emerson's steamboat, which was a step of man into discord and oblivion, he has to make many other realities and to hold them together in his person.

A precise illustration of man's struggle against nature is offered by American literature. The American phenomenon remains unexplained, unless we consider its heritage of knowledge, wisdom and power, transplanted to a new, huge territory and still kindled and irritated by the resistance of virgin unexplored realities.

Although they were few, the first settlers had in them not only the European past, but also the whole spiritual purpose of western civilization. The flow of immigrants and the multiplication of the race then gave birth to one nation, but more important than the nation is the spirit. The millions of square miles and the millions of inhabitants have no meaning, the only value there is the creative, invisible action of the spirit struggling against wild, formless, dumb, cruel nature; a spirit stronger, greater, richer than nature. Though the thread uniting the Americans to their forefathers was frail, they inherited the spirit of a great civilization.

The material side of American civilization dazzles even the Americans themselves, but we should not forget that it is the weakest side. We forget that millions of men and of square miles cannot destroy a single living idea. The decisive factor in the amazing growth of America is neither geographical nor demographical, it is the presence of a pugnacious spirit. But this spirit, however rich and many-sided it may be, remains invisible, so that we are left wondering what we call the facts : cranes and tractors, towns and dams, banks and farms. The spirit is behind, invisible, but is it not faintly apparent in the literature of the U.S.A.?

Literature, of course, is not the only source, but we can safely assume that it is one of the main roads leading to the

L

discovery of the spirit, if we are able to separate the time-bound elements from the timeless ones. I know that a history of literature is a safe and reliable guide, but it will mislead us if we are concerned with the spirit, not with the word. It is easier to deal with the visible and at times more immediately rewarding, manifestations of the mind, provided that we are not confined to them.

The time-bound elements, in any literature, are those that fade with time, lose their freshness, appeal to a past generation, and leave us indifferent. When we study an ancient literature as the remnant of a lost civilization, we are sometimes unable to find the gems among the rubbish because we have lost the taste that would enable us to appreciate them. On the contrary, when we are dealing with a living literature, and sympathizing with it, as I intend to do with American literature, if only we raise our individual tastes to a universal level, we partake of the taste that presides over that literature. Universal, not collective, for a collective taste is always time-bound. Contemporary Americans are impatient with Cooper's lengthy discourses, or with the lack of action in Henry James's novels : this collective reaction is not to be entirely trusted; the modern taste for dynamic plots and a colloquial style suits the cinema better than the novel, and represents a certain trend in a definite period.

The historian of literature finds it difficult to place contemporary writers because he lacks the perspective of the future. For the philosopher of literature, the problem is quite different. The great danger is that he is involved in a time-bound trend, and has not a universal taste.

We admire the artistic mastery of the cave-paintings of Lascaux or Altamira, even if we can only conjecture their meaning. We lose something of their spirit, but what we understand is certainly universal and timeless! A deep culture together with a great power of comparison is therefore essential to the philosopher of contemporary literature. No work escapes the verdict of universal taste.

Vague, as it is, the word 'taste' is fitted for a philosophy of literature. There is no better criterion. We know that Cooper or Hawthorne are old-fashioned, not only in their language, but also in their style and in their problems; at the same time we take it for granted that the American spirit, the universal spirit, is in them. They mix the ridiculous and the boring with the everlasting and living elements. In many of their words there is a voice that we can hear.

All writers are contemporaries. In spite of all historical changes, we must read them as if they were sitting in our armchair; for a writer it is not important to be French, to live in the seventeenth century with a powdered face and a wig and a king appointed by God. It is much more important to have one's plays performed in the twentieth century.

Few American writers stand the test of time, and those who do come nearer to Socrates than to Billy Graham.

Whatever may be the traditions and the achievements of American literature its chief task is to look for and to affirm its identity, for what are traditions and works that are not your own, that are not created?

34. THE SEARCH FOR IDENTITY IN AMERICAN LITERATURE

THE word 'identity' is ambiguous, but there is no choice. I mean : the quality of being distinct from any other literature, of having a personality (if a literature may have a personality). The title : "The search for personality . . ." would be misleading, since it would suggest that American writers are individually striving at acquiring a personality.

But identity does not mean only a differentiation from other existing literatures—a kind of segregation which, as we shall see, was particularly painful to achieve and which still has its victims and its opponents—identity also means the cultural consequence of the occupation of the American soil. We have to distinguish roughly three phases in this struggle for cultural autonomy : the colonial or New-England phase, characterized by its puritanism and by being a mere extension of Great Britain; the European phase, characterized by the assimilation of European movements such as romanticism, realism and socialism, and the present American phase, characterized by focusing on American problems in an American way.

These three phases are held and driven by one dynamic force, the search for identity. "Who am I" and "where am I" are relevant questions for the American. The paradox of possessing a new huge territory but no language and no cultural background of their own is the basic fact : the Americans have to invent a way of life and a way of thinking just when they are becoming the leaders of the world. Deeply rooted in the European foreign tradition which they must make their own, they have jumped into uninherited economic and political self-sufficiency and power. There is no doubt a disconnection between their dismembered culture and their standardized way of life. How far they will be able to fill the gap is a matter of conjecture. The only way of finding an answer is by studying their successive attempts at assessing their identity in literature.

The problem is much simplified if we place it on a philosophical basis. As I have advanced in the first part of this book, identity in literature is nothing but the final identity between the spirit and nature or, to apply this equation to American literature, between the spirit of the nation and its material circumstances.

In an extremely busy civilization that exalts efficiency, dynamism, material power and individual success, that is averse from the contemplative attitude and mistakes technique, hygiene and progress for righteousness, there is little scope for spiritual activities; I mean that these activities are not integrated, although some of them, particularly those of the churches, receive a kind of official consecration.

The Americans, like any other man, are by no means deprived of spiritual abilities, but what I claim is that the exercise of these activities remains *marginal*. It is neither prohibited nor stifled nor made to run on rails, it is simply superfluous, and the result is that it is distorted in two directions: either it aims at recognition, and in that case apes and flatters fashion and material power, or it denies any value to the present civilization, and creates a world of its own without any connection with the hated environment and even deliberately opposed to the tenets of society.

Jesus' education and spiritual struggles, symbolized by his temptations in the desert, were in some degree in harmony with the environment; his life and his teachings give a meaning to the past, the present and the future. American writers and divines, on the contrary, are priests of a lost religion. Society feigns to recognize them, and gives them money—the only thing such a society has to give but the grants, the funds, the scholarships, the fellowships, the Bibles and the State or industrial prizes will not create a single writer, a single grain of spirit.

Divines, writers and artists have to be successful, and then nothing but money is to be found at the bottom of their works; or else they have to work apart from society, to be outcasts, mandarins, abstruse scholars, or to belong to some 'lost generation'.

The force of this dilemma is noticeable from the very beginning of American literature. James Fenimore Cooper, who was really the first novelist to deal with American themes (if we except Châteaubriand's lurid descriptions of Luisiana) already introduces the type of the absent-minded, lost scholar in *The Prairie;* as for his Indians, what are they if not, through their metaphorical language, the poetry of America, the link with the soil? Where there is action in his novels, it is mainly illustrated by the theme of flight; on expanding the meaning of such a choice, we may come to the conclusion that American life is a perpetual fight, an escape from stability, from static, contemplative life : it is an uprooted and uprooting life. The popularity of Dumas' novels among American students is significant of this love of action, change and movement, still prompted by the puritanical desire to improve oneself.

Washington Irving, one of the fathers of American prose, looked for his theme either outside America or in a legendary past, and elaborated them in a polished, elegant style which had no connection with the style of life of his contemporaries.

Hawthorne, who spent part of his life in Europe, felt, when he was writing his masterpiece, *The Scarlet Letter,* that he had to shut himself up in the past of New England like a hermit, in order not to be distracted by the teeming new life which was changing the face of his country. It is also significant that Thomas Wolfe, who was looking for a father, for a home, like James, discovered his America by comparison in Europe.

Like any other literature, American literature aims at

authorship, authenticity and individual self-sufficiency, an ambition that cannot be fulfilled unless the whole population of the country contributes to it. The fact that Washington Irving found recognition among his compatriots shows that his apparently artificial tales found an echo in the American heart.

The split in the personality of the American writer has none the less been accentuated in later generations. There is a constant tradition of cultural emigration. Henry James and T. S. Eliot not only found it necessary to visit Europe, but also became British citizens. The opposite trend, symbolized by Mark Twain's *The Innocents Abroad* is a reaction too violent to hide the split : it looks like the counterpart of its opposite. The identity is not yet won, although much has been acquired and made by hard toil and ingenious skill. The American is still tempted, either to forget his heritage or to shut himself up; to become either the natural man in the newest car or the sophisticated hermit.

That the American mind is able to create is sufficiently evident, and it is continuously creating itself, but a whole, balanced and coherent identity is its special aim.

All national cultures have the same need for a balance between heritage, foreign influence and self-affirmation,[1] and above all between creative activities and production, but what is secondary for many of them is a question of existence for American culture. The fact that the United States have become the greatest power in the world increases their need for assimilating their inherited culture. What they need is not novelty, but coherence.

[1] The plight of Switzerland, a country with *various* national cultures, may be recalled in this connection.

35. THE SMILE OF THE SPIRIT

My analysis of a passage from *Wuthering Heights* shows clearly that the meaning is neither in the words uttered by the character nor in the plot, neither in the opinions of other characters nor those of the narrator, neither in the author's art nor in the reader's impressions. The meaning consists of the interplay of all these factors and results from successive attempts at penetration, composition and integration.

However composite the meaning may be, it aims at unity. Indeed, strong unity can only be achieved when widely different materials are used, so that the chances of success and of failure increase with the difficulties of the attempt. A short poem, let us say a quatrain, may be pungent, clear, sharp, and surprising, but the sudden certainty it creates leaves a residue of doubt. The aim of art is not to detach a fragment of reality, to isolate it from its context and to mould it into a unique form, making it static and definitive. The form of a poem or of a statue is static and definitive, but the form is not all. The aim is unity, a living unity capable of radiating its own essence and achieved only when foreign elements have been assimiliated and tend to propogate their similitude. Art must contain contrasts, contradictions and raw materials, and blend them together. Here we arrive by way of logic and experiment at a conclusion which, in the first part of the present book, was rather presented as an axiom: the rule of unity. Unity is neither of life nor of nature, it is of the spirit. It is the law of art, for the function of art is to assimilate life and nature, to impose a meaning upon them. No trace of the spirit can be found in nature, and whatever meaning, whatever unity is to be found in nature will come from man's own spirit. You cannot find them unless you have them, unless you create them. The world is a virtual metaphor, it is penetrated, inhabited and lived in a process of comparison. The world becomes a work of art in which you live, the more so as its unity admits of much diversity. Attraction and assimilation are what gives life and freedom.

This thesis has been illustrated by the search for identity in American literature. One of the recurrent aspects of the American literary endeavour seems to me to be the assimilation, on the one hand of the Western heritage, on the other hand of the new circumstances. In this, American literature illustrates one peculiar aspect of the human adventure. From the point of view of the philosopher of literature, history appears as a huge effort at assimilation. If man is to realize his aims and his needs, nature must become art, and that event is still far off. The spirit must create order. A work of art, with its unity and its meaning, is a modest contribution to order, yet the writer knows at least that, without meaning, there is no reality; a delicate and incomplete meaning is better than nothing. Each man, as I have stated in the first part, bears the responsibility—the meaning—for his life, and with him the spirit is at stake more than his individual life. The writer is not alone, nor should he believe that he owes his works to his individual effort; the individual has no value unless he becomes the universal; *he is one when he is all.*

In writing on the cultural heritage of the Pilgrim Fathers, I have tried to suggest what that 'all' means, how invisible and yet inescapable the spirit is : it is not in a few elect, but in every one, in those who are unknown as well as in those in whom the spirit sleeps.

To conjure up the presence of some spirit is always a positive achievement, even if that spirit shows itself only in a faint smile. Such is the achievement of all works which have even a slight shade of meaning, such is the only criterion authorizing us to set any value for a work. Once more I am

compelled to show this presence of the spirit in one text. I
have voluntarily refrained from casting my net over any great
masterpiece, for my purpose is precisely to evoke a faint
smile :

> "By degrees Rip's awe and apprehension subsided. He
> even ventured, when no eye was fixed upon him, to taste
> the beverage, which he found had much of the flavour of
> excellent Hollands. He was naturally a thirsty soul, and
> was soon tempted to repeat the draught. One taste provoked
> another; and he reiterated his visits to the flagon so often
> that at length his senses were overpowered, his eyes swam
> in his head, his head gradually declined, and he fell into a
> deep sleep."[1]

The reader need not think of the context and of the meaning of the story (though it is quite a significant tale, for it
deals with the changes produced by American independence).
Here is Rip, a drunkard. There are various attitudes towards
a drunkard and thousands of ways of dealing with the subject. Irving, who, as can be seen, handles history firmly and
rhythmically, has chosen the attitude of benevolent condescen-
sion in a way that produces the faint smile. 'Naturally a thirsty
soul' is a pregnant phrase, 'naturally' being used as an explanation, 'thirsty soul' graciously transforming the excesses
of the body into virtues of the soul. The irony is mild, and the
spirit resides in this moderation, for moderation also may
imply harmony.

I have insisted on one particular aspect of this passage, and
yet those who have read other tales by Irving will admit that
the same effect recurs, as if all the characters and all the stories
were attended by a smiling angel. It is the imperceptible presence of the spirit. Other writers are able to display it more
powerfully and more evidently, but even with Irving there is
no doubt; the spirit is there, throwing a weak light on a

[1] *Rip Van Winkle,* by Washington Irving.

limited reality, but still doing something in the way of understanding, penetrating and assimilating.

That presence of the spirit is the ultimate reality in a tale
of which neither the characters nor the plot are taken very
seriously. Besides, that presence resides as much in the reader,
who experiences an awakening of his spirit, as in the author
who evokes that presence. Something intangible has been communicated, something invisible is shared, something that does
not exist, but lives, acts and sees, something that does not
belong to anybody, but to which things and people belong.

Rip at least belong to the spirit; his objective reality is
merged into, led and dominated by an angel who is more real
than himself. Irving's spirit is not satisfied with an excursion
in the destitute realm of existence : it is entirely master of its
materials, though Irving does not claim to catch much and
even plays with the reader's credulity. Yet Irving has more
fantasy than invention, and most of his tales have very
creditable sources. There is just enough likelihood in Rip for
the reader to give credit to the story, but the important thing,
in this tale as well as in more ambitious works, is the presence
of the spirit, a presence compensating for the loneliness, discord and loss of existence.

36. THE SKYLARK

HARMONY and assimilation are essential features of poetic truth and they apply to all literary forms, though they are more easily analysed in dramas and novels than in other forms of expression. They are least easily analysed in poetry, for, in a poem, they are poetry, and almost nothing can be detached from them. There is even one element of the poem, the image, the function of which is to harmonize and to assimilate.

Much has been written recently on poetic imagery, and modern poets tend to use metaphor freely, a freedom made possible by the general indifference towards poetry, the only means of expression that totalitarian régimes do not think it worth while to oppress. The great danger for poetry is not its lack of perfection so much as its futility. Poetic violence, like any sort of violence, is a sign of weakness. It is not sufficient to express a state of mind in rhythmical and musical words, and to invest it with surprising metaphors; the goal, here more than in other literary forms, is to fuse these elements into an indissoluble harmony. I have even observed, in my analysis of a passage from *Wuthering Heights,* that this indissolubility is the characteristic of poetry.

Now indissoluble harmony should not be mistaken for static form, nor dynamism for vagueness. If I may contribute to the discussion of poetic imagery, I should like to emphasize its aspect as a living force, and, correspondingly, its efficiency, for it seems to me that nothing is more in danger and more necessary today than the efficiency of the spirit.

When dealing with the phenomenon of literary creation I noted that the writer cannot create out of nothing. He creates

a harmony that places us in another sphere than that of existence. Poetic harmony must involve the sphere of existence and
in so doing must take its place, annihilate it. It is vain to
argue that our existence is what it is, for, if poetry exists, our
existence is no longer what it is! To a large extent, the
metaphor is the instrument of that transformation. A study of
the metaphor may show the virtues of efficiency (assimilation)
and unity (harmony) in poetry.

Metaphors, similes, allegories, symbols, parables, etc., are
poetic comparisons. The function and the necessity of comparison can be explained by the following considerations : It is
possible to build a perfect system of ideas with little reference
to realities and without thinking of its applications. Conversely,
it is possible for the historian to accumulate thousands of irrefutable facts without his works having any meaning. These
opposite extremes, a system in the void and a meaningless
series of documents, are possible when no relation is allowed
between facts and ideas; they are the perfect antithesis of
poetry.

The relation between facts and ideas, as I have repeatedly
shown, is meaning, and though meaning is arrived at through
successive attempts at harmony, yet there is a short cut, the
poetic comparison. Certain poems, made up of comparisons
and sustained by a powerful exaltation, vibrate from beginning to end. Such is Shelley's *To a Skylark*.[1] I may be
wrong and partial, but in spite of his defects and limitations,
Shelley is the English poet I love most. No other succeeds in
communicating such warmth of heart. As for his metaphors,
the least I can say is that they are living, and this characteristic
makes them poetic. A very clever metaphor is not necessarily
poetic; it may be clever and at the same time dry without
ceasing to be good. The most pertinent and exact metaphors are
often lifeless and static; I would even go as far as to say that a
certain dose of madness and imprecision allows a metaphor

[1] The consistency of some similes in this poem is demonstrated in *Seven
Types of Ambiguity*, by William Empson (London, Chatto &
Windus, 1953, p. 156-161).

to vibrate. At any rate, a metaphor, to be living, to be poetic, must be capable of transmitting its vibrations to wider spheres. Such is the effect of Shelley's metaphors; but where shall I choose? A quotation from such a poem as *To a Skylark* is like an unnecessary surgical operation, when the body is healthy; yet I must perform it, and here I have dissected out an organ, from which the blood flows on both sides:

> "From rainbow clouds there flow not
>   Drops so bright to see,
> As from thy presence showers a rain of melody."

This composite metaphor (rainbow—skylark) is chosen neither for its exactitude nor for its cleverness. It is hardly logical at all, a rational analysis (which would here be stupid) would show where the comparison does not work; and yet what are the logic and the exactitude of science compared with the harmony and the reality of this indissoluble whole? The effect of this metaphor (I insist on the poem being an *act*) is that nature is seen and felt as a moving harmony. Is nature harmonious? I do not know what nature is, but I am certain that Shelley has made—and still makes—a harmonious nature. If it were confined to nature, that harmony would be no harmony at all, for the condition of harmony is to propagate itself and to be broken and negated by the first obstacle. Shelley dares the obstacle. From the skylark, the harmony radiates from the physical world into the soul. How unjust was my quotation! This small addition will repair the damage and cause a new injustice:

> "Waking or asleep,
>   Thou of death must deem
> Things more true and deep
>   Than we mortals dream,
> Or how could thy notes flow in such a crystal stream?"

'Crystal stream' is no original metaphor. A crystal stream of notes is hardly more ingenious, but, here as always, the poetry is in the whole, in the crowning metaphor of the musical transparency of death. In prose, this looks preposterous. The metaphor does not sound healthy, and the poet is mad. There is, however, a superior logic in his madness (just as there is a fundamental unreason in reason), a logic with which the romantics were supremely familiar, the logic which demands that harmony shall be complete and infinite, measure be boundless, music be flowing and limited things be *limitlessly significant*. This makes *To a Skylark* a beautiful poem. It is not the skylark that is beautiful, but the living and musical significance invented by Shelley. Invented? We feel that it comes from Shelley's soul like a pre-existing idea. Yet such a boundless measure is not for us; we come short of truth, love and joy, and we are always seeking them, however erratically we may progress towards the final goal. We will always listen to the skylark and always pay attention to harmony where we find it. That is a warning to, or a solace for young poets. Here is the last stanza :

> "Teach me half the gladness
>   That thy brain must know,
> Such harmonious madness
>   From my lips would flow,
> The world should listen then, as I am listening now."

Why does Shelley listen to the skylark, and why do we listen to Shelley? Because both provoke a response. We cannot remain indifferent to harmony. Cool-headed and full-blooded, Shelley very consciously terms it 'harmonious madness'. A highly logical madness, the very antidote to the two extremes of discordant reason : the system in the void and the meaningless series of documents.

37. PLENITUDE OF THE PRESENT, OR
THE HEART OF LITERATURE

I DO not try to interpret the poem. Read the whole poem; it will give you more than I can. Nor shall I analyse the whole net of metaphors and other images. The skylark has always been seen as a symbol of elevation, music and joy, but the poet makes something different out of this established symbol; choose, for example, from all the skylarks in English poetry, *The Sea and the Skylark,* by Gerard Manley Hopkins; in that the uninterrupted music of words (alliteration and assonance in combination with rhyme and rhythm) is like a coat of many colours: Hopkins points at the sky with an ivory cane, but Shelley carries us upward. Shelley's sky is in us. His harmony surges freely and widely, knowing no barrier of confinement and dogma; Hopkins is baroque in this sense: his poems are precious pearls distilled within a shell, gorgeous life attached by a silk thread; they shine as brightly as Shelley's rainbow drops, but they are hard jewels, and our response is checked, for their brightness comes from a strange light. In this:

> ". . . We, life's pride and cared-for crown,
> Have lost that cheer and charm of earth's past prime!"[1]

there is an allusion to Christian theology. I raise no objection to religious poetry, and I note a definition of poetry by Ramuz: "La poésie, c'est le sentiment du sacré". I observe, however, that there is a separation between substance and

---

[1] Last line of the first tercet and first line of the second tercet of Hopkins's sonnet.

176

meaning in Hopkins, that all the music of the world will not give life to a fixed system, and that the meaning of the poet cannot be that of the theologian, the philosopher or the scientist, for, again, the meaning of the poet is characterized by its wholeness and its power of radiation; its meaning is life, life made a vibrating whole instead of being reduced to its elements.

Shelley dissolves the hard core of life and needs no silk thread. Like all poets, he has his limitations, and some of his ideas stand like a foreign body within his poetry, but his meaning keeps the crystal transparency that permits the eye to move freely from the centre to the outer spheres of waves.

Hopkins was welcomed by the younger generation for several reasons, including the wrong one : his variety and the successive strata of his meaning show signs of disintegration. Attempting to cope with the discrepancies of modern life, the 'modern' poets are forced to welcome raw materials, whereas the romantics were fortunate enough to live in a time when ideas and enthusiasm allowed them to look through the past and the future without caring much for the discordant present.[2] Though it was dangerously ideal, their vision was more harmonious, and we are still invited to listen to them as Shelley listened to the skylark, while our poor contemporary poets (the present writer is one of them) cannot expect to receive so much attention, for their harmony is pierced with the discordant shouts which they are honest enough to hear.

All poets of all times strive at plenitude ('harmonious madness'), a plenitude made finite in the poems and made possible by a radiating power that shakes and assimilates the obstacle, the raw materials. Our study of poetry, especially of the metaphor, from the point of view of its harmony, shows that the function of a short cut to meaning like the metaphor is not simply to link together two points of comparison or two orders of existence, for instance the order of nature and the order of

[2] It should be recognised, however, that some contemporary writers try to cope with the present time and all its implications. Joyce's *Ulysses* is a symbol for this remarkable trend.

feelings. From the distinct, static, intellectual and more or less logical frame or net of relations there emerges a living whole with the continuity of real time. The whole interplay of metaphors in our first quotation :

"From rainbow clouds there flow not
Drops so bright to see,
As from thy presence showers a rain of melody."

is in a state of flux. According to Bergson, the intellect by itself, being analytical, is unable to catch the reality of time, so that what he calls the artistic perception must contribute, for art is experience.[3] Time is the unknown, continuous, unseizable substance cut into moments, methodically framed by the mind and finally penetrated by the poetic experience. It is the most difficult thing to assimilate, so that the poet, even as he provokes the sense of the flight of time (one of the common and classical themes), despairs at the same time from stopping it. But he knows how to prolong a state of mind, a perception and a reality, he even succeeds in making a moment eternal.[4] The past and the future, melting into each other, are illusions; only the present is real, the eternal present, the seen, conceived, redeemed and transfigured present, not the static eternity.

The short cut to meaning, the metaphor, is representative of the whole poetic truth. Comparison, transposition, creation, transfiguration, expression, etc., are parts of it, but only the whole matters, and the whole is made of a living harmony. The meeting of the eye and the object is a remarkable event;

[3] "La vérité est qu'une existence ne peut être donnée que dans une expérience. Cette expérience s'appellera vision ou contact, perception extérieure ne général, s'il s'agit d'un objet matériel; elle prendra le nom d'intuition quand elle portera sur l'esprit. Jusqu' où va l'intuition? Elle seule pourra le dire." *La Pensée et le Mouvant,* Genève, Skira, 1946, p. 56.
[4] See the chapter on resurrection.

strange is the dialogue between the visible landscape and the invisible state of mind, but the wonder begins when the moment, the present meeting, becomes eternal, extending its waves of meaning beyond all limits, from the troubled emotional centre of the moment.

That the skylark is no 'blithe spirit' we know well, and when we are disappointed with the bird seen near us on the ground we think that the poets personify things too easily. But what if those unexisting persons live; what if our heart is a skylark? Things otherwise impossible happen in poetry. Shelley's vision of liberty was not a reality reserved for future men, but remains in our heart. The invisible, unexisting thing called heart is itself a metaphor, a meaning in one word, a radiating centre. Is it not the life-giving light and warmth, so whole and impatient of limits that when hurt it hates the obstacle, a spot on its light? Does the laborious development of our philosophy lead us back to the simple truth known to all but the sophisticated, that evil begins when a thing is done without heart?

A lack of harmony, too, goes with an absence of the heart, with a lack of participation, with no radiating power of joy and love, the only fruit-bearing power. The reader of this book is familiar with two pleas, the one against spiritual authority, the other against intellectual objectivity; and he will perhaps permit the following remarks, bearing upon the heart of our philosophy of literature.

Detachment and objectivity are often praised as virtues. In the first part of this book I have claimed that there is no such thing as a pure object, the very term 'object' implying the corresponding subject. I can now go further, and add that intellectual detachment and pure objectivity (these things do not exist, but they are presented as ideal attitudes) imply a fundamental dryness of the heart. We hear them generally praised as virtues, and indeed there remains in them a flavour of the rationalistic struggle against uncontrolled emotions, but reason without laws is madness too, and there is a fanaticism of reason. The attitude of detachment, though often necessary, is always sterile, and the only way of coping with things is to participate in them. I have sufficiently proved, first, that such participation explains the freedom of the writer in face of his object, secondly, that no fictitious character is real unless it is made of a joint participation of the model (objective truth), the other characters, the author, the readers, etc., and thirdly that not only the truth of moral beings, but physical existence and the presence of the spirit come from the fundamental concord between things and spirit. Understanding is penetration.

As to my plea against spiritual authority, I may add that if poetry is concentrated, not diluted, made of harmony and indescribable vibrations, then no authority, however transcendental it may be, should replace the life-giving centre, the heart. The heart is too often replaced by an institution, the authority of which steals from the heart its very substance, a blood-sucking, life-robbing, time-annihilating authority, however spiritual it may claim to be! There is no abstract Love with capital letters. Love is nothing if not in man's hearts, now and forever, but especially now; we divide time, but truth, the real time, is in the immediate and infinitely expanding present.

Such a reality of time, as opposed to a concept of time, such a time made one with the feeling of time, is most real in works of art, in which the thing and the perception of the thing are one, and especially in those literary works where the immediate presence of the spirit is felt.

We have all experienced the peculiar exaltation caused by music. I have once noted—this a matter of feeling and cannot be proved—that a characteristic of this musical exaltation is the creation of an expanding musical space, as if time (the medium of music more than of any other art) were made one, present without the barriers of past and future, and were invaded by the waves of rhythm and melody, which in turn become a new, real, though unexisting, space.

This new, all-pervading present, in which we participate in exaltation, a more or less abnormal state, is a creation of art. It is made possible by the unity of feeling and matter.

Perhaps we can live without music, but only when moved by music to a state of exaltation can we live, be real, and be what we are. It is no use saying that art is artificial; creation is the only means of saving ourselves from unreality and of attaining the truth in whose face the eyes of *our* spirit shine.

A complete consciousness would involve a knowledge of the future. The future remains unknown, and we associate it with a feeling of insecurity, as if the future were less stable than the past.

What is unstable is the separation between past, present and future, as well as the separation between the future—or the past—and the immediate ego.

The present is the time I—or my contemporaries, or 'we'— feel, and the present is real when the past and the future are felt at the same time.

Of course it would be a double contradiction to say that we are conscious of the past and of the future, first because we live in neither and are not physically present in them, secondly because consciousness makes a distinction between past, present and future, so that the present is essentially what we live in and what we experience, whereas the past and the future exist outside this narrow consciousness.

Yet no time can be said to exist without any consciousness, and even when dividing, distinguishing, analysing, comparing and measuring, consciousness does not stop the flow of continuity. Literature is a means of catching the concrete unity of duration.

It is not time that limits literature, but literature that breaks the limits of time, links apparently unrelated events, renews the past and appeals to posterity.

Barriers, frontiers, division, political parties and short-sightedness are strengthened by the shortness of human life, by the fixity of institutions and by the passivity and laziness of those who inherit prejudices without trying to get rid of them. But time gnaws at the borders and blurs the outlines. Time is a flux, the universal, never-ending stream in which no drop is for long allowed an individual existence. The walls fall : only the whole remains, and the whole resides in each sentient atom. The repeated pettiness of life and the assertion of exclusive opinions make a gap in the plenitude of reality, introduce a closed lie in the open truth. The moment is no fragment of time, the real moment is always, otherwise how could life be caught in one poem? The longest book tells nothing unless it has as its germ one unique perception. Like the fully grown plant, it is all contained in one original cell.[5] A book may display a great variety, show contrasts and even contradictions, progress along different ways and end violently; its greatness is not there, but in the smallest, original cell where all its life resides. Its beauty, its suggestiveness, its logic and its style contribute to its unity; in proportion as it develops and extends it becomes one spaceless unit of life, a life that, at least in the best books, is not material, though matter is present in it. The spirit (there is no better word) laughs at small things, scorns the big ones and imposes its measure; it is life's very heart, which admits of no division.

In art as elsewhere, the function determines the value, and a misunderstanding—in most cases a narrowing—of the function provokes the corresponding distortions of values. One of the broadest functions of art consists in manifesting awareness. Another definition of art : conscious representation. Whether art should be figurative or not is a false problem, for it is impossible either to avoid any representation or merely to represent a supposedly external world (as if objectivity were absolute). The real difficulty is to unite those two divergent directions of art : towards the inside (the spirit) and towards the outside (the objects).

When painters like Corot and Turner want to convey the

---

[5] This statement perhaps recalls Sir Herbert Read's notion of " organic form."

impression of a certain light, for instance of the early sunset, or of a haze, they have to compose extremely subtle shades of colour, so that a certain atmosphere intervenes between the landscape and the onlooker. Behind these shades and behind the artist's awareness of these subtleties is the presence of a man, as important as the presence of the landscape. The value of the paintings lies in the harmony between these two presences. However little the artist may be aware of them and however insufficient his means of expression may be, his work will be precious if the landscape and the man are one, for we see countless things, are aware of many and become few.

Awareness is the spring of literature, too, an awareness that creates its object. There is as little greatness in pure awareness as in rigorous objectivity. Both are in fact impossible, and the difficult balance between these opposite extremes is rarely achieved. The presence of the author is always felt, but how far does that presence correspond to the thing he says? Conversely, the most significant events are uninteresting until they speak with a voice that can be understood.

Events exert an influence on literature and literature on events, but the world of immediate happenings and the longings of the soul are too intrinsically different from each other to react directly and completely upon each other. There is a communication between them in literature, which appeals both to the soul and to the world, an intermittent and incomplete communication by means of which the soul becomes actual and the world real.

The world and the soul are so distant—and yet so much in need of each other—that they live (if, as I maintain, life is made simultaneously of things, beings, and of the feelings towards things and beings) in their exceptional meeting in literature.

Literature may be considered as a means of communication, not only between man and the world, but also between men. It is a fragile and inadequate means of communication, yet it is a solid and true link when a sense of unity is conveyed.

Literature holds a central place among human activities; a radiating and harmonizing centre, it maintains the balance. In an age of spatial, nuclear and psychological exploration it should be remembered that all the ways of communication would meet in literature if the meaning of words were not distorted by conflicting ideologies and propagandas. The present lack of equipoise between dreams and action, science and religions, politics and common sense, technique and human welfare, etc., increases the need for a restoration of meaning.

We are all strangers in a strange world. In the way from man to man and from man to the world, there is the irreplaceable bridge of literature across abysses of ignorance, servitude and confinement. May all men enjoy creative freedom and be one in the Word!

INDEX